English 2200

SECOND EDITION WITH INDEX

A Programed Course in Grammar and Usage

JOSEPH C. BLUMENTHAL

HARCOURT BRACE JOVANOVICH, INC.

New York   Chicago   San Francisco   Atlanta   Dallas

THE SERIES

ENGLISH 2200

ENGLISH 2600

ENGLISH 3200

Tests for English 2200

Tests for English 2600

Tests for English 3200

TEACHER'S MANUAL for Each Textbook

ABOUT THE AUTHOR

Joseph C. Blumenthal received his A.B. and A.M. degrees from the University of Michigan. He also did graduate work at the University of Chicago and at Columbia University. From 1938 to 1959 he was Head of the English Department at Mackenzie High School in Detroit. He is now devoting his full time to textbook writing. Among his writings are the *Common Sense English* series, the *English Workshop* series (with John F. Warriner and others), and *The English Language* series (with Louis Zahner and others).

ABOUT THE SECOND EDITION

The inclusion of an index in this edition is intended to make ENGLISH 2200 more useful to students and teachers by giving them ready access to the entire body of material treated in the text. Each entry in the index is listed by frame number and page to facilitate its location in the text.

THE TEST BOOKLET

A 60-page Test Booklet designed for use with English 2200 consists of a Pre-test, two Mastery Tests for each of the eleven units, and a Final Test.

Printed in the United States of America

ISBN School Printing: 0-15-313995-1
     College Printing: 0-15-522700-9
Library of Congress Catalog Card Number: 76-1413

TO THE STUDENT

ENGLISH 2200 is a programed course in grammar, sentence-building, correct usage, and punctuation. A new feature of this edition is an index which can help you locate a particular topic quickly when you need it for reference or review.

If this is your first experience with a programed textbook, you may be puzzled by its appearance. As you leaf through its pages, you may wonder why it looks so different from other books you have studied.

Why the zebra-like pages with alternating bands of gray and white?

Why is the material divided into small bits or *frames*?

Why don't you read the pages from top to bottom as you do other books?

Why are the answers printed in the marginal strips where they can be so easily seen?

ENGLISH 2200 looks so different because it is built upon some modern learning principles. For many years, the problems of learning have been studied scientifically in colleges and universities all over our country. As a result, new discoveries have been made which can make learning faster, surer, more thorough (and, we hope, more fun). **ENGLISH 2200** is based on some of the most important of these discoveries.

1. In a programed course, often called simply a *program*, the material is broken down into very small and carefully arranged steps—approximately 2200 in this book—through which you reason your way, one step at a time. There is no separation between explanation and exercise, as in other language textbooks; the two are tightly interwoven. Every step, or *frame*, calls for a written response, which requires both *thinking* and *concentration*. The advantages of "reasoning your own way" instead of "being told" have been known to good teachers ever since the days of Socrates. By thinking your way through the program, you are likely to understand better and to remember longer.

2. Programs are constructed to prevent mistakes before they happen. The psychologists call this "errorless learning" and have proved its importance by scientific experiment. The steps are so small and their arrangement is so orderly that you are not likely to make many errors. When an error occurs, you catch it immediately by turning the page for the answer. You are corrected before a wrong habit can become established. You spend your time *learning*—not *unlearning*. Using a programed textbook is like having a private teacher who watches you as you work and who sets you back on the track the moment you wander off.

3. A very important factor in this method is what the psychologists call *reinforcement*. Its importance in learning cannot be stated too strongly.

With the usual textbook, you first study the lesson (which you may or may not understand completely). Then you apply what you have studied to an exercise. Unfortunately, you do not find out until some time later (often the next day) whether you did the exercise correctly. With **ENGLISH 2200** you discover immediately whether your answer is right or wrong. At this point something very interesting and mysterious happens. The instant you find out you are right, the idea "takes root," so to speak, in your brain. This does not happen as successfully when time (even a moment or two) is allowed to elapse before you discover that you are right.

Finding out immediately that you are right is called *reinforcement*, and the quicker and more often this happens, the better you learn and re-member. A reinforcement is something like a reward; and if you have ever taught a dog tricks, you know from experience how the biscuits speed up learning.

4. With programed instruction you can advance at your own speed. Since you work by yourself, no one needs to wait for you, and you don't need to wait for anyone else. Many students complete an entire course of study in a fraction of the time usually required by the traditional text-book method. The time you save by this method can be used profitably in other language activities.

How to Use **ENGLISH 2200**

Each step (or frame) requires that you perform some operation. For ex-ample, in many of the frames you will do one of two things:

1. If there is a blank line, write in the missing word or letter.

Example: Jones is the name of a *person*.

2. If there are two or more words or letters in parentheses, underline the correct answer.

Example: Jones is the name of a *(person, place)*.

(*Note:* Your teacher will tell you whether to write your answers in this book, in a notebook, or on sheets of paper.)

The first work frame is Frame 2 (on page 3). After you complete Frame 2, turn to Frame 3 *in the same position* on the next *right-hand* page (page 5). In the column to the left of Frame 3, you will find the correct answer to Frame 2. If your answer is not correct, turn back and correct it before doing Frame 3. You will always find the answer to a frame in the column to the left of the frame that you are to do next. Thus you find the answer to Frame 3 to the left of Frame 4, the answer to Frame 4 to the left of Frame 5, and so on.

Go completely through the book, taking only the top gray frame on each *right-hand* page (3, 5, 7, 9, 11, etc.) until you reach the end. When you reach the end of the book, turn back to page 1 and follow the second band —a white one—through the book, still working only on the *right-hand* pages. Then proceed to the third horizontal band, which is gray, going through all the *right-hand* pages. Continue in this way through the fourth, fifth, and sixth bands. When you come to the last white band on the last *right-hand* page (Frame 1128), turn back to page 2 and start reading the gray bands at the top of the *left-hand* pages. Continue through the book, following each horizontal band through the *left-hand* pages. The last frame is 2249 on page 372.

The alternating bands of white and gray will make it easy for you to stay on the same horizontal band as you advance through the book. Since both frame and answer are numbered (each in the lower right corner), you will always know where you are and where to go next.

Getting the Most from **ENGLISH 2200**

1. Whenever you are unsure about the correct answer to a frame, read the frame again very carefully, looking for clues. You will generally find a clue that guides you to the right answer. As the lesson advances, fewer and fewer clues will be given; so if you make a mistake, you will need to go back a few frames to try to correct your thinking. If you still don't understand where your mistake lies, ask your teacher for help.

2. Take as much time as you need in figuring out your answer. But once you write your answer, turn immediately to the next frame to check its correctness. Scientific experiment has proved that the more quickly you check your answer, the better you learn. *Even the delay of a few seconds makes a big difference!*

3. Don't cheat yourself out of the valuable experience of thinking! Don't look at the answer in the next frame until *after* you have figured it out for yourself. Thinking things through takes effort, but it is this kind of effort that results in the most effective kind of learning. You are not working for grades on these lessons because the lessons will not be scored. In fact, you will always end with a perfect score because you are expected to correct each error immediately (and you will probably make very few). However, your teacher may want to evaluate your work by administering and scoring the tests that accompany **ENGLISH 2200.** "Peeking ahead" for the answer will not give you the reasoning ability you will need to pass the tests.

If you will use **ENGLISH 2200** in the mature way in which it is designed to be used, you may discover that, working at your own pace, you have achieved a better command of the fundamentals of your language—and in a much shorter time. You may also find that you have developed your ability to think and concentrate in ways that will help you in your other studies. You will have profited from letting science help you with its most recent and exciting discoveries about how people learn.

JOSEPH C. BLUMENTHAL

CONTENTS

Lesson **1** We Must Have Nouns

[Frames 2-25]

---

some

Underline the one pronoun:

The *dog* **with the black** *spots* **is** *mine.*

188 | 189

---

relationship

Lesson **13** Prepositions Make Useful Phrases

376

[Frames 378-403]

---

given, gave

Write the correct past forms of **give:**

Bob _____ **away all the stamps that his friend** *had* _____ **him.**

564 | 565

---

taken, run

Mr. Potter (*gave, give*) **us some unusual roses that he had** (*grown, grew*) **in his backyard.**

752 | 753

There's

There (*were, was*) **several planes circling the airport.**

940 | 941

No
 	
1128
	The object forms of pronouns are used for the direct objects of verbs.
	They are also used for the objects of prepositions.
	
	     a. **The class voted for** *her*.
	     b. **The class elected** *her*.
	
	In which sentence is *her* the object of a preposition?____
	
	1129

If ... afternoon 1315	**The dog chewed up the letter before Dad had read it.** The adverb clause starts with the clause signal _____ and ends with the word _____. 1316
Yes 1502	Can a clause stand by itself as a sentence? (*Yes, No*) 1503
cabin. Uncle 1689	**As we were working very hard at chopping down weeds on Saturday afternoon Uncle John drove up.** _____ 1690

Yes
 	
1876
	We often put an address right after a name, with no preposition such as **at, in, on,** or **of** to tie it in. Then we surround even a one-part address with commas.
	
	     a. **Write to the Royal Hotel in** *Miami* **for reservations.**
	     b. **Write to the Royal Hotel** *Miami* **for reservations.**
	
	In which sentence should two commas be used? _____
	1877

"Has the dog been fed?" asked Mother. 2063	Here is the same quotation at the *end* of the sentence: **Mother asked, "Has the dog been fed?"** This entire sentence is not a question. It merely contains a question. To show that the quotation is a question, we put the question mark (*inside, outside*) the quotation marks. 2064

In grammar, we study different kinds of words. We learn how these words are fitted together to mean something. The study of words and the way they are put together is called *gr*_____.

Note to student:
Do not write in your book without your teacher's permission.

2

---

mine

189

To be a sentence, a group of words generally needs to have both a *subject* and a _____.

190

In the previous lesson, you saw that every preposition is followed by a noun or pronoun.

The name *of* the colt was Smoky.

The preposition *of* is followed by the noun _____.

378

---

gave, given

565

PRESENT	SIMPLE PAST	PAST WITH HELPER
pull	**pulled**	**(have) pulled**
paint	**painted**	**(have) painted**
see	**saw**	**(have) seen**

All the above verbs are regular except the verb _____.

566

---

gave, grown

753

I had (*wrote, written*) a letter but had (*threw, thrown*) it out.

754

---

were

941

(*Where are, Where's*) **the books for our class?**

942

a 1129	a. **The dog followed** *him*. b. **The dog walked behind** *him*. In which sentence is *him* the object of a preposition? _____ 1130
before ... it 1316	Lesson **45** **Putting Adverb Clauses to Work** [Frames 1318-1346]
No 1503	An adverb clause does the job of an _____. 1504
afternoon, Uncle 1690	**He went through the cabin then he began to laugh.** _____ 1691
b 1877	Punctuate this sentence: **The Filmcraft Shop 88 Main Street repairs cameras.** 1878
inside 2064	Punctuate this sentence: **Mother asked Has the dog been fed** 2065

grammar 2	To talk or write to other people, we need many different kinds of words. For example, we need names for all the things we see around us. Underline two words that are the names of things in this room: **wall tree chair moon** 3
verb 190	**The boat drifted away from the dock.** The verb in this sentence is ———————. 191
colt 378	The noun or pronoun that follows a preposition is called the **object of the preposition.** **The name *of* the colt was Smoky.** The object of the preposition *of* is the noun ———————. 379
see 566	Lesson **19** Seven Irregular Verbs [Frames 568-604]
written, thrown 754	**Philip (*run, ran*) to the phone and reported what he had (*seen, saw*).** 755
Where are 942	**How much (*was, were*) the rides at the carnival?** 943

b

1130

a. **The police blamed ....**
b. **... won three games.**

Which sentence would require the subject form of the missing pronoun? ____

1131

In one way, a sentence and a clause are alike. Both have a subject and a verb. However, there is one big difference between them. A clause (*can, cannot*) stand by itself.

1318

---

adverb

1504

An adjective clause does the job of an _____.

1505

---

cabin. Then

1691

His amusement puzzled us   did he think that we had done a poor job?

_____

1692

Shop, Street,

1878

Dates, just like addresses, can also have more than one part.

    a. **On** *Monday, June 27,* **we start for Seattle.**
    b. **On** *Monday* **we start for Seattle.**

In which sentence does the date have more than one part? ____

1879

Mother asked,
"Has the dog
been fed?"

2065

Punctuate this sentence. Notice that the quotation is a question:

      How is the fishing   Bert asked

2066

wall, chair 3	Underline two words that are the names of foods: **cloud** **bread** **lettuce** **cement** 4
drifted 191	When we change a sentence from present to past time, or from past to present time, the word that usually changes is the _____. 192
colt 379	**The store** *around* **the corner sells school supplies.** In this sentence, the object of the preposition *around* is the noun _____. 380

	Look at the simple past forms of the seven verbs we shall study in this lesson:
	
	    SIMPLE PAST: **drove** **spoke** **took** **fell**
	                     broke **wrote** **ate**
	Do any of these simple past forms end in *–ed*? (*Yes, No*)
	
	568

ran, seen 755	**The bell** (*rang, rung*) **before we had** (*sang, sung*) **our school song.** 756
were 943	(*Where are, Where's*) **the bag of apples?** 944

b 1131	a. John met ... at school. b. ... met John at school. Which sentence would require the object form of the missing pronoun? ____ 1132
cannot 1318	a. **our <u>town</u> <u>is</u> small** b. *although* **our <u>town</u> <u>is</u> small** Which one of these word groups should start with a capital letter and end with a period because it is a complete sentence? ____ 1319
adjective 1505	a. **when, while, because, if, although, unless** b. **who (whom, whose), which, that** Which group of clause signals are used to start adverb clauses? ____ 1506
us. Did 1692	**He finally controlled his laughter then he gave Dad and me the shock of our lives.** _____ 1693
a 1879	We punctuate dates just as we do addresses. After you write the first part of a date, put a comma both *before* and *after* each additional part. Punctuate this sentence: **On Friday August 3 1492 Columbus set forth on his historic voyage.** 1880
"How is the fishing?" Bert asked. 2066	Now punctuate this same sentence turned around: **Bert asked How is the fishing** 2067

bread, lettuce	Underline two words that are the names of living things:
	man **stone** **window** **horse**
4	5

verb	PRESENT: **Phyllis often writes me letters.**
	If you changed this sentence to past time, you would need to change the word _____ to _____.
192	193

corner	a. **The seat** *behind* **Jerry was vacant.**
	b. **The seat** *behind* **him was vacant.**
	In which sentence is the object of the preposition *behind* a pronoun? ___
380	381

No	SIMPLE PAST: **drove** **spoke** **took** **fell**
	broke **wrote** **ate**
	The past forms of these verbs do not end in *–ed*, as most verbs do. They are therefore (*regular, irregular*) verbs.
568	569

rang, sung	**After we had (*ate, eaten*) our lunch, we (*set, sat*) and talked for a while.**
756	757

Where's	(*Was, Were*) **these pictures taken at school?**
	Note to student:
	You are now ready for Unit Test 4.
944	945

a

1132

Dave lives with *them.*

We use the object form of the pronoun because it is the object of the preposition _____.

1133

---

a

1319

a. **Our town is small.**
b. *although our town is small*

When we add the clause signal *although* to sentence *a*, the sentence becomes a _____.

1320

---

a

1506

a. **I read a book** *which my friend recommended.*
b. **I read a book** *because my friend recommended it.*

Which sentence contains an adverb clause? _____

1507

---

laughter. Then

1693

This wasn't Uncle John's cabin   it belonged to the Fosters.

_____

1694

Friday, 3, 1492,

1880

Punctuate this sentence:

I was born on Saturday December 8 1951 in Cleveland.

1881

Bert asked,
"How is the
fishing?"

2067

Compare a quotation that is an exclamation with one that is a question:

    a. **"How is the fishing?" Bert asked.**
    b. **"What an enormous fish!" Bert exclaimed.**

There is only one difference: Where sentence *a* has a question mark, sentence *b* has an _____ point.

2068

man, horse	Underline two words that are the names of persons: **pencil Frank desk Judy**
5	6
writes, wrote	**My friend very seldom sees his grandparents.** The verb in this sentence is _____.
193	194
b	A group of words that begins with a preposition and ends with its object is called a **prepositional phrase**. A prepositional phrase would need to have at least _____ words. (How many?)
381	382
irregular	Now let's look at the helper forms of these same verbs: **(have) driven (have) spoken (have) taken (have) fallen** **(have) broken (have) written (have) eaten** Each of these helper forms ends with the two letters _____.
569	570
eaten, sat	**He had** (*gone, went*) **to the office and had** (*spoken, spoke*) **to the manager of the store.**
757	758
were	UNIT 5: **USING THE RIGHT MODIFIER** Lesson **32** **Choosing Between Adjectives and Adverbs**
945	*page 11* [Frames 947-973]

with 1133	The words that generally change their form when they are moved from the subject to the direct object position are (*nouns, pronouns*). 1134
clause 1320	**The stores were closed.** Underline the clause signal that could turn the above sentence into an adverb clause: **all because yesterday** 1321
b 1507	A clause that modifies a noun or a pronoun is called an _____ clause. 1508
cabin. It 1694	**During the past winter, one cabin had been torn down** **therefore Uncle John's cabin was now the third from the road.** _____ 1695
Saturday, 8, 1951, 1881	In this and the following frames, add commas for addresses and dates wherever they are needed. If no commas are needed, make no changes. **We shall stop at Topeka Kansas for one day.** 1882
exclamation 2068	a. **"What an enormous fish!" Bert exclaimed.** b. **Bert exclaimed, "What an enormous fish!"** By putting the exclamation point inside the quotation marks, we show that the (*quotation, sentence*) is an exclamation. 2069

Frank, Judy	Underline two words that are the names of places: sugar airport London coat
6	7

sees	Can a verb consist of more than one word? (*Yes, No*)
194	195

two	Between the preposition and its object, you will often find words that modify the object. **We sent a plant** *with many large pink flowers.* How many words stand between the preposition and its object? _____
382	383

–en	Here are the three basic forms of the verb **drive**. PRESENT SIMPLE PAST PAST WITH HELPER drive drove (have) driven We say, "Dad *drove* us to school," but we say, "Dad *had* _____ us to school."
570	571

gone, spoken	**I had (*ran, run*) into some barbed wire and had (*tore, torn*) my best shirt.**
758	759

	Do you remember that adjectives modify nouns and pronouns? **James is polite.** The word **polite** is an adjective because it modifies the noun _____.
page 13	947

pronouns 1134	Two pronouns do not change their form when they are moved from the subject to direct object position. These two pronouns are (*she, you, it, they*). 1135
because 1321	*because my brother plays the piano* This is an adverb clause. It could be changed to a sentence by dropping the clause signal _____. 1322
adjective 1508	ADJECTIVE CLAUSE SIGNALS: **who (whom, whose), which, that** All these adjective clause signals are pronouns. When the pronoun is the subject of the verb in the adjective clause, use the subject form (*who, whom*). 1509
down. Therefore 1695	**We then moved over to Uncle John's cabin which we found in very bad condition.** _____ Note to student: You are now ready for Unit Test 8. 1696
Topeka, Kansas, 1882	**We shall stop at Topeka for one day.** 1883
quotation 2069	Now we are ready to turn to another problem. Here is a quotation that continues for several sentences without interruption: **"The score was tied. We had two outs. There was a man on third," explained Ricky.** Is each sentence surrounded by quotation marks? (*Yes, No*) 2070

airport, London	Can you talk about anything that doesn't have a name? (*Yes, No*)
7	8
Yes	Underline two helping verbs in this sentence: **It has been raining all morning.**
195	196
three	**My grandmother taught in a very small country school.** How many words stand between the preposition and its object? _____
383	384
driven	Write the two past forms of **drive:** **Art _____ as though he** *had* **_____ all his life.**
571	572
run, torn	**We** (*seen, saw*) **several uniforms that had been** (*worn, wore*) **in the Battle of Gettysburg.**
759	760
James	Adjectives can modify only nouns and pronouns. They cannot modify verbs. **James answered politely.** In the above sentence, **politely** tells *how* about the verb _____.
947	948

you, it 1135	a. **I, he, she, we, they** b. **me, him, her, us, them** In which group are the object forms of the pronouns? ____ 1136
because 1322	**if while because although** If you put one of these words at the beginning of a sentence, would it still be a sentence? (*Yes, No*) 1323
who 1509	ADJECTIVE CLAUSE SIGNALS: **who (whom, whose), which, that** When the verb in the adjective clause already has another word as its subject, use the object form (*who, whom*). 1510
cabin, which 1696	UNIT 9: **LEARNING TO PUNCTUATE** Lesson **59** **End Marks of the Sentence** [Frames 1698-1721]
No commas 1883	**We selected Friday June 17 as the date for our party.** 1884
No 2070	**"The score was tied. We had two outs. There was a man on third," explained Ricky.** Only one set of quotation marks ("—") is needed although this quotation continues for _____ sentences. (How many?) 2071

No	You can't talk about anything unless it has a _____.
8	9

has been	Underline two helping verbs in this sentence:
	Someone must have taken my coat.
196	197

	When you hear or read a preposition, you are not satisfied until its object comes along to complete its meaning.
four	a. **in a** c. **in a very few**
	b. **in a very** d. **in a very few minutes**
	Which is a completed prepositional phrase? ____
384	385

drove, driven	Underline the correct form of the verb:
	We *have* (*drove, driven*) **to Chicago many times.**
572	573

saw, worn	It (*began, begun*) **to rain after we had** (*driven, drove*) **only a few blocks.**
760	761

	James answered politely.
answered	The word **politely** doesn't modify a noun or pronoun. It modifies the verb **answered.**
	Is **politely** an adjective? (*Yes, No*)
948	949

b	Write the subject form of each of these pronouns:
	me _____
	him _____
1136	1137

	I remembered the answer ... *I had turned in my paper.*
No	Underline the clause signal that would make the best sense in the above sentence:
	because so that after where
1323	1324

	Underline the correct pronoun:
whom	**The lady** (*who, whom*) **came to the door was very pleasant.**
1510	1511

	Every sentence needs a mark of punctuation to show that it has ended. The three end marks are a period (.), a question mark (?), and an exclamation point (!).
	Is a comma one of the end marks that can show the end of a sentence? (*Yes, No*)
	1698

| Friday, 17, | **We selected June 17 as the date for our party.** |
| 1884 | 1885 |

	One set of quotation marks ("—") will take care of any number of sentences as long as the quotation is not interrupted.
three	Add the missing quotation marks:
	The bus swerved. It missed the dog. The passengers praised the driver for his skill, said Harold.
2071	2072

name 9	In grammar, we have a special name for any word that is used to name a *person, place,* or *thing.* We call such a word a **noun.** A noun is a word used to _____ a person, place, or thing. 10
must have 197	Underline two helping verbs in this sentence: **The plane should be arriving soon.** 198
d 385	a. **for an entire** c. **for a long, tiresome** b. **for my mother** d. **for a very young** Which is a completed prepositional phrase? ____ 386
driven 573	a. **My dad ... the same car for eight years.** b. **My dad** *has* **... the same car for eight years.** In which sentence would *drove* be the correct verb?____ 574
began, driven 761	**Del must have** (*knew, known*) **that the price was soon going to** (*rise, raise*). 762
No 949	Besides adjectives, we also have adverbs. Do you remember that many adverbs are used to tell *how* about the action of the verb? **James answered politely.** The word that tells us how James **answered** is the adverb _____. 950

I he 1137	Write the subject form of each of these pronouns: her _____ us _____ them _____ 1138
after 1324	... *Lincoln had little formal schooling,* **he was highly educated.** Underline the clause signal that would make the best sense in the above sentence: **Until Although If Unless** 1325
who 1511	Underline the correct pronoun: **One girl** (*who, whom*) *we invited* **couldn't come.** 1512
No 1698	Put a period (.) after a sentence that states a fact. This is what most sentences do. a. **The rain flooded the streets** b. **Did the rain flood the streets** One sentence states a fact; the other asks a question. Which sentence should end with a period? ____ 1699
No commas 1885	**Edwin Drake first struck oil near Titusville Pennsylvania on August 27 1859.** 1886

"The bus...
skill,"
 	
2072
	When you write conversation, start a new paragraph each time the speaker changes.
	    "Why are you stopping?" I asked.
	    "The light just turned red," replied Joe.
	    "That's a very good reason," I laughed.
	This conversation requires _____ paragraphs. (How many?)
	
	2073

name 10	A word that is used to name a person, place, or thing is called a _____. 11
should be 198	a. I *did* **solve the problem.** b. I *did* **the problem easily.** In which sentence is *did* used as a helping verb? ____ 199

b
 	
386
	To find where a prepositional phrase begins, always look for a preposition.
	
	    a. **to, from, by, in, with, of, near**
	    b. **was, this, our, there, top, all**
	
	The words that can start prepositional phrases are those in group ____.
	
	387

a 574	PRESENT SIMPLE PAST PAST WITH HELPER **break** **broke** **(have) broken** We say, "I *broke* my pencil," but we say, "I *have* _____ my pencil." 575
known, rise 762	**Our neighbors** (*did, done*) **nothing about the branches that had** (*fell, fallen*) **into our yard.** 763
politely 950	Here are only a few of many, many adverbs that tell *how* about the action of a verb: **cleverly** **cheerfully** **proudly** **bravely** **timidly** All the above adverbs end with the two letters _____. 951

she we they 1138	Write the object form of each of these pronouns: he _____ they _____ 1139
Although 1325	**We lived ...** *there were very few stores.* Underline the clause signal that would make the best sense in the above sentence: **although as where while** 1326
whom 1512	The *two* adjective clause signals that can be used to refer to persons are (*who, which, that*). 1513
a 1699	Also put a period after a sentence that gives a command or makes a request. a. **Shut off the motor.** b. **Please open the door for me.** Which sentence makes a request? ____ 1700
Titusville, Pennsylvania, 27, 1886	**We drove on November 24 from El Paso to Phoenix.** 1887
three 2073	"Look at that cloud," said Dave. "It looks just like a big fish," said Paul. "To me it looks just like one more cloud," said Jack. "You have very little imagination," commented Paul. How many paragraphs does this conversation require? _____ 2074

noun 11	Underline two nouns in this sentence: **The boy became an artist.** 12
a 199	**is, am, are — was, were, been** These six words are all forms of the verb (*be, do, have*). 200
a 387	Underline the prepositional phrase: **Bob's answer to the question was correct.** 388
broken 575	Write the two past forms of **break**: **Jerry** _____ **his record after I** *had* _____ **mine.** 576
did, fallen 763	**Our neighbor** (*came, come*) **over and** (*brung, brought*) **us some vegetables from her garden.** 764
–ly 951	There are many words that have both an adjective and an adverb form: ADJECTIVES: **clever cheerful proud brave** ADVERBS: **cleverly cheerfully proudly bravely** The words that end in *–ly* are _____. 952

him
them

1139

Write the object form of each of these pronouns:

I _____

we _____

she _____

1140

---

where

1326

I wrote a note to myself ... *I would remember my appointment.*

Underline the clause signal that would make the best sense in the above sentence:

so that   until   since   because

1327

---

who, that

1513

Underline the correct pronoun:

The teacher (*who, which*) **directs our band can play every instrument.**

1514

---

b

1700

a. **Sign your name here**
b. **Did you sign your name**

Which sentence should end with a period because it gives

a command? ____

1701

No commas

1887

Helen Cummings 3417 Ashton Road was a witness to the accident.

1888

---

four

2074

Beginning with this frame, each sentence contains a *direct* quotation. Copy each sentence, adding the necessary punctuation and capitalization. (Use an exclamation point only when the frame directs you to do so.)

The clerk replied   we don't accept checks

2075

boy, artist	**The boy became an artist.** Both underlined nouns in this sentence are the names of (*persons, places, things*).
12	13
be	A word that receives the action of the verb or shows the result of this action is called a *direct* _____.
200	201
to the question	Underline the prepositional phrase: **My cousins live in another city.**
388	389
broke, broken	Underline the correct form of the verb: **Mr. Thomas** *had* (*broken, broke*) **his glasses.**
576	577
came, brought	**I had** (*swam, swum*) **the length of the pool ten times and had** (*begun, began*) **to feel tired and hungry.**
764	765
adverbs	Adjectives can modify only nouns and pronouns. Adjectives cannot modify verbs. Should you ever use an adjective to tell *how* about the action of a verb? (*Yes, No*)
952	953

so that

1327

... *you do something about your spelling,* **you can't expect it to improve.**

Underline the clause signal that would make the best sense in the above sentence:

Because   When   As if   Unless

1328

---

who

1514

The *two* adjective clause signals that can be used to refer to things and animals are (*who, which, that*).

1515

---

a

1701

a. **Dave signed the letter**
b. **Sign the letter**
c. **Did you sign your name**
d. **Please sign this letter**

Every one of these sentences should end with a period except sentence ____.

1702

Cummings, Road,

1888

On May 1 1884 the first skyscraper was started in Chicago Illinois.

1889

The clerk replied, "We don't accept checks."

2075

We are flying over Houston   announced the pilot

_____

_____

2076

persons

13

Underline two nouns in this sentence:

Chicago has many parks.

14

---

object

201

Is every action verb followed by a direct object? (*Yes, No*)

202

---

in another city

389

Underline the prepositional phrase:

The road around the mountain is narrow.

390

---

broken

577

a. **The hot water** *has* ... **the glass.**
b. **The hot water** ... **the glass.**

In which sentence would *broke* be the correct verb? ____

578

---

swum, begun

765

They (*throwed, threw*) **out all the records that had been** (*broke, broken*) **by the children.**

766

No

953

a. **clever**   **cheerful**   **proud**   **brave**   **timid**
b. **cleverly**   **cheerfully**   **proudly**   **bravely**   **timidly**

To tell *how* about the action of a verb, use the words in group ____.

954

a. **I, he, she, we, they**
b. **me, him, her, us, them**

In which group are the pronouns in the subject form? ____

1142

Unless

1328

The coach spoke ... *he expected to win.*

Underline the clause signal that would make the best sense in the above sentence:

until   as though   so that   after

1329

---

which, that

1515

Underline the correct pronoun:

The farmer showed us a calf (*who, that*) **was only a week old.**

1516

---

c

1702

If a sentence states a fact, gives a command, or makes a request, end it with a _____.

1703

1, 1884, Chicago,

1889

Phil recently took a job with the Pacific Oil Company of San Diego.

1890

"We are flying over Houston," announced the pilot.

2076

The librarian said   you will like this book

_____

_____

2077

Chicago, parks 14	**Chicago has many parks.** Both underlined nouns in this sentence are the names of (*persons, places, things*). 15
No 202	a. **The captain shouted loudly.** b. **The captain shouted his orders.** In which sentence is the action verb **shouted** followed by a direct object? ____ The direct object is _____. 203
around the mountain 390	Underline the prepositional phrase: **My dad came home with several large boxes.** 391
b 578	PRESENT SIMPLE PAST PAST WITH HELPER **speak** **spoke** **(have) spoken** We say, "Tom *spoke* to the principal," but we say, "Tom *has* _____ to the principal." 579
threw, broken 766	**Our cat was (*lying, laying*) in a box that we had (*sat, set*) on our back porch.** 767
b 954	a. **James is . . . .** b. **James answered . . . .** In which sentence should you use the adverb **politely**? ____ 955

a 1142	Underline the correct pronoun: (*He, Him*) **went to the game.** 1143
as though 1329	WHEN? **while, when, whenever, as, before, after, since, until** HOW? **as if, as though** **Some people break out in a rash** ... *they eat strawberries.* To start the clause in the above sentence, you would select a clause signal from the (WHEN? HOW?) group. 1330
that 1516	In this and the following frames, combine each pair of sentences. Change the italicized sentence to the kind of word group indicated in the parentheses. Make no change in the other sentence. *I turned on the hose.* **No water came out.** (adverb clause) _____ 1517

period
 	
1703
	Put a question mark **(?)** after a sentence that asks a question.
	    a. **That direction is north**
	    b. **Which direction is north**
	Which sentence should end with a question mark because it asks a question? ____
	
	1704

No commas 1890	**The first telephone call between New York and San Francisco took place on January 25 1915.** 1891
The librarian said, "You will like this book." 2077	**This corn was just picked said the farmer** _____ _____ 2078

places 15	Underline two nouns in this sentence: **The key was in the lock.** 16
b orders 203	a. **School opened on Monday.** b. **The children opened the package.** In which sentence is the action verb **opened** followed by a direct object? ____ The direct object is _____. 204
with several large boxes 391	Underline the prepositional phrase: **Our hike through the woods was exciting.** 392
spoken 579	Write the two past forms of **speak**: **Doris _____ to me after I** *had* _____ **to her.** 580
lying, set 767	**Dr. Kirk had** (*gave, given*) **Judy strict orders to** (*lie, lay*) **quietly in bed for several days.** 768
b 955	a. **Richard <u>writes</u> very cleverly.** b. **Richard <u>is</u> very clever.** In which sentence does the verb show action? ____ 956

He 1143	**He** <u>went</u> to the game. We use **He,** the subject form of the pronoun, because it is the subject of the verb _____. 1144
WHEN? 1330	WHERE? **where, wherever** WHY? **because, since, as, so that** ... *Nancy had grown so much,* **we could hardly recognize her.** To start the clause in the above sentence, you would select a clause signal from the (WHERE? WHY?) group. 1331
When (As, Although) I turned on the hose, no water came out. 1517	**Sue can play the piano.** *She has never taken lessons.* (adverb clause) _____ _____ 1518
b 1704	Punctuate these two sentences: **I have two sandwiches_____ Do you want one_____** 1705
25, 1891	Lesson **66** Unit Review [Frames 1893-1913]
"This corn was just picked," said the farmer. 2078	**Mr. Grove repeated our test will be tomorrow** _____ _____ 2079

key, lock 16	**The <u>key</u> was in the <u>lock</u>.** Both underlined nouns in this sentence are the names of (*persons, places, things*). 17
b package 204	a. **The train stopped the traffic.** b. **The train stopped for a few minutes.** In which sentence is the action verb **stopped** followed by a direct object? ____ The direct object is _____. 205
through the woods 392	**This is a poem about a beautiful spring day.** In this sentence, the prepositional phrase begins with the preposition _____ and ends with its object _____. 393
spoke, spoken 580	Underline the correct form of the verb: **The Turners** *have* (*spoke, spoken*) **about going to Mexico.** 581
given, lie 768	**Grandmother had** (*drunk, drank*) **her tea and had** (*lain, laid*) **down to rest.** 769
a 956	Underline the correct modifier: **Richard writes very** (*clever, cleverly*). 957

went	Underline the correct pronoun: (*I*, *Me*) **went to the game.**
1144	1145

WHY?
 	
1331
	WHEN? **while, when, whenever, as, before, after, since, until**
	WHERE? **where, wherever**
	   Mother hid the candy ... *none of us could find it.*
	
	To start the clause in the above sentence, you would select a clause signal from the (WHEN? WHERE?) group.
	
	                                                          1332

Sue can play the piano although (though) she has never taken lessons. 1518	*I was reading a magazine.* **I rode past my stop.** (adverb clause) _____ _____ 1519

sandwiches.
one?
 	
1705
	To be polite, we often put a request in the form of a question rather than a command. Since we are not asking a question that requires an answer, we could use a period.
	
	      a. **Does this window open?**
	      b. **Will you please repeat the question?**
	
	We could use a period after sentence ____. 1706

	In this review lesson, you will find the story of Fritzie, a very sensitive dog. Add the commas that are needed, according to the rules you studied in this unit. Several sentences do not require commas. Also put an end mark—a period, a question mark, or an exclamation point—at the end of each sentence. (*Turn to the next frame.*) 1893

Mr. Grove repeated, "Our test will be tomorrow." 2079	**You owe me a quarter** **Kip reminded me** _____ _____ 2080

things 17	You can see or touch most of the things that nouns name but not all of them. Underline *one* word that names something you *cannot* see or touch: **door desk freedom** 18
a traffic 205	Underline the direct object: **Gary wrote his name in the book.** 206
about, day 393	**I stepped over the sleeping dog very carefully.** In this sentence, the prepositional phrase begins with the preposition _____ and ends with its object _____. 394
spoken 581	a. **Judy** *had* **. . . about her hobbies.** b. **Judy . . . about her hobbies.** In which sentence would *spoke* be the correct verb? ____ 582
drunk, lain 769	**Dad** (*laid, lay*) **some newspapers on the grass and** (*laid, lay*) **down to relax.** 770
cleverly 957	**Richard writes very cleverly.** We use the adverb **cleverly** because it tells *how* about the action of the verb _____. 958

I 1145	**I** <u>went</u> to the game. We use **I**, the subject form of the pronoun, because it is the subject of the verb _____. 1146
WHERE? 1332	ON WHAT CONDITION? **if, unless, although, though** HOW? **as if, as though** ... *you will read the poem again,* **you will like it better.** To start the clause in the above sentence, you would select a clause signal from the (ON WHAT CONDITION? HOW?) group. 1333
Because (While, As) I was reading a magazine, I rode past my stop. 1519	**We found a store.** *It was having a sale.* (adjective clause) _____ _____ 1520
b 1706	a. **Will you please shut off the water?** b. **Will the store refund your money?** After which sentence could we use a period because it is really a request rather than a question? ____ 1707
	The Hunters have lived at 32 Calvert Avenue Glendale Cali- fornia for many years 1894
"You owe me a quarter," Kip reminded me. 2080	**Are you going to play asked Floyd** _____ _____ 2081

freedom 18	freedom courage imagination These nouns are not the names of persons, places, or things. They are the *names of ideas* we have in our minds. Can we talk about these ideas just as we can talk about *teachers, schools,* or *books*? (Yes, No) 19
name 206	Underline the direct object: **I took my camera to school yesterday.** 207
over, dog 394	**The weather on my last birthday was rainy.** The prepositional phrase begins with the preposition _____ and ends with its object _____. 395
b 582	PRESENT SIMPLE PAST PAST WITH HELPER **write** **wrote** **(have) written** We say, "Stan *wrote* for a sample," but we say, "Stan *has* _____ for a sample." 583
laid, lay 770	**I** (*lay, laid*) **aside my books and** (*lay, laid*) **down on the sofa.** 771
writes 958	You have seen that many modifiers have two forms: one without *–ly* and another with *–ly*. To describe the action of the verb, you would use the form (*with, without*) *–ly*. 959

went 1146	**He** _went_ to the game.　　**I** _went_ to the game. Now let's put these two sentences together by using a compound subject: 　　　_____ **and** ____ **went to the game.** 1147
ON WHAT CONDITION? 1333	WHERE?　**where, wherever** HOW?　　**as if, as though** 　　　　**Dick played** ... _he were very tired._ To start the clause in the above sentence, you would select a clause signal from the (WHERE? HOW?) group. 1334
We found a store which (that) was having a sale. 1520	**A lady sat next to me.** _She was holding a baby._ (adjective clause) _____ (Are you changing the italicized sentences?) 1521
a 1707	a. **Will this train leave on time?** b. **Will you kindly let me know if you can go?** After which sentence could we use a period? ____ 1708
Avenue, Glendale, California, years. 1894	**On Tuesday July 17 two policemen came to their door** 1895
"Are you going to play?" asked Floyd. 2081	**Just look at your shoes　　exclaimed Mother** (Use an exclamation point.) _____ 2082

Yes	**freedom courage imagination** Because these words are the names of ideas in our mind, they are called _____.
19	20

camera	Underline the direct object: **Many explorers have lost their lives in the Arctic.** Note to student: You are now ready for Unit Test 1.
207	208

on, birthday	**I kept my collection in a large wooden box.** The prepositional phrase begins with the preposition _____ and ends with its object _____.
395	396

written	Write the two past forms of **write**: **Paul** _____ **to his uncle after he** *had* _____ **to his parents.**
583	584

laid, lay	**Don had** (*laid, lain*) **his skates where someone might have** (*fallen, fell*) **over them.**
771	772

with	a. **Dave spoke** *proudly* **of his team's success.** b. **Dave was** *proud* **of his team's success.** In which sentence does the verb show action? ____
959	960

He, I

1147

He <u>went</u> to the game.   I <u>went</u> to the game.

He and I <u>went</u> to the game.

When we combine these two sentences, do we use the same forms of the pronouns? (*Yes, No*)

1148

HOW?

1334

Adverb clauses are useful for combining sentences. The clause signal shows how the facts or ideas are related.

a. **The field was muddy. We decided to play.**
b. *Although the field was muddy,* **we decided to play.**

Which arrangement shows more clearly how the two facts are related? ____

1335

A lady who (that) was holding a baby sat next to me.

1521

We followed our friends. *We hoped to overtake them.* (*–ing* word group)

_____

_____

1522

---

b

1708

Put an exclamation point (**!**) after a sentence that expresses sudden or strong feeling, such as *fear, surprise, anger, disgust,* or *delight.*

   a. **The storm was terrible**   b. **It rained slightly today**

Which sentence would you end with an exclamation point to show your strong feeling about the weather? ____

1709

Tuesday, 17, door.

1895

A neighbor it seems had reported them to the police for beating their dog

1896

"Just look at your shoes!" exclaimed Mother.

2082

What took so much time   **asked Betty**

_____

_____

2083

nouns
 	
20
	Underline *one* noun that is the name of an idea:
	
	    Sylvia **equality** **gym** **elevator**
	
	    21

lives 208	UNIT 2: **WORDS THAT ENRICH THE SENTENCE** Lesson **8** **Adjectives Make Pictures** [Frames 210-240]
in, box 396	Some words can be used as either prepositions or adverbs. If the word has an object, it is a preposition. Otherwise, it is an adverb that modifies the verb. **The crowd traveled on.** Is the word *on* followed by an object? (*Yes, No*) 397

wrote, written
 	
584
	Underline the correct past form of the verb:
	
	    Terry *has* (*written, wrote*) **a very good story.**
	
	    585

laid, fallen 772	**My parents had** (*rose, risen*) **early and had** (*flew, flown*) **to Washington.** Note to student: You are now ready for Unit Test 3. 773

a
 	
960
	Underline the correct modifier:
	
	    Dave spoke (*proud, proudly*) **of his team's success.**
	
	    961

Yes

1148

We seldom hear anyone except small children say, "*Him* went to the game" or "*Me* went to the game." However, we do sometimes hear grown-ups say, "*Him* and *me* went to the game." Is this the same mistake? (*Yes, No*)

1149

---

b

1335

---

a. **Ted played the radio** *while I was trying to study.*
b. **Ted played the radio. I was trying to study.**

Which arrangement shows more clearly how the two facts are related? ____

1336

We followed our friends, hoping to overtake them.

1522

I looked at his face. **I wondered if he was serious.** (*–ing* word group)

_____

_____.

1523

---

a

1709

---

a. **We missed the bus.**
b. **We missed the bus!**

Which sentence shows stronger feeling? ____

1710

---

neighbor, seems, dog.

1896

Did the neighbor or anyone else ever see them beat Fritzie

1897

"What took so much time?" asked Betty.

2083

Aunt Helen screamed   don't sit on my cake

(Use an exclamation point.)

_____

_____

2084

equality 21	Underline *one* noun that is the name of an idea: **grocer farm tree honesty** 22
	Up to this point, you have studied three kinds of words: *nouns, pronouns,* and *verbs.* **I want to buy a pencil.** In this sentence, the word *pencil* is a _____. 210
No 397	**The crowd traveled** *on.* Because the word *on* modifies the verb **traveled**, it is an _____. 398
written 585	a. **We ... several themes this semester.** b. **We** *have* **... several themes this semester.** In which sentence would *wrote* be the correct verb? ____ 586
risen, flown 773	UNIT 4: **SUBJECT AND VERB MUST AGREE IN NUMBER** Lesson **26** **Recognizing Singular and Plural Subjects** [Frames 775-808]
proudly 961	Underline the correct modifier: **You must swing the bat more** (*vigorous, vigorously*). 962

Yes	It seems strange that people who use single pronouns correctly will make mistakes when they use pronouns in pairs.
	
	     a. *He* **and** *I* **lost our way.**
	     b. *Him* **and** *me* **lost our way.**
	
	Which sentence is correct? ____

1149	1150
a	In this and the following frames, change each italicized sentence to an adverb clause. Select a clause signal that will make the meaning clear. Write the clause only. *I took the clock apart.* **I couldn't put it together again.** ———————————————————————————, **I couldn't put it together again.**
1336	1337
Looking at his face, I wondered if he was serious.	**Unfortunately, my birthday comes on December 26.** *It is the day after Christmas.* (appositive word group) ——————————————————————————— ———————————————————————————. (Remember that an appositive word group does not ordinarily have a subject and a verb.)
1523	1524

b	Single words and groups of words that express strong feeling are often written as sentences and punctuated with exclamation points.
	
	    Horrors! A snake! **Oh, what a beautiful day!**
	
	Punctuate the following:
	    Hurray____ A home run____

1710	1711
Fritzie?	**No he never actually saw them beat the dog or mistreat him**
1897	1898
Aunt Helen screamed, "Don't sit on my cake!"	## Lesson 73 Unit Review
2084	

honesty 22	Underline *one* noun that is *not* the name of an idea: **happiness fairness motor beauty** 23
noun 210	If you said to a clerk, "I want to buy a pencil," he would probably ask you, "What kind?" If you said, "I want a red pencil," the clerk would immediately get you a pencil because the word _____ describes *what kind* of pencil you want. 211
adverb 398	a. **The crowd traveled** *on*. b. **The crowd traveled** *on* **the train.** In which sentence is the word *on* used as a preposition? ____ 399
a 586	PRESENT SIMPLE PAST PAST WITH HELPER **take** **took** **(have) taken** We say, "They *took* the wrong road," but we say, "They *have* _____ the wrong road." 587
	Singular means "one"; **plural** means "more than one." The noun **road** is singular; the noun **roads** is _____. 775
vigorously 962	a. **Bob was very** *foolish* **with his money.** b. **Bob spent his money very** *foolish*. Which sentence is *not* correct? ____ 963

a 1150	We frequently use pronouns in pairs. When doubtful about which pronoun to use, "split the doubles" like this: **(She, Her) and (I, me) planned the party.** SPLIT: *She* planned the party. *I* planned the party. Underline the same pronouns in the combined sentence: *(She, Her)* **and** *(I, me)* **planned the party.** 1151
After (When, Although, If) I took the clock apart, 1337	*Mike plays the trombone.* **All the neighbors always close their windows.** ————————————————————————, **all the neighbors always close their windows.** 1338
Unfortunately, my birthday comes on December 26, the day after Christmas. 1524	**Rip Van Winkle slept for twenty years.** *He is the main character.* (appositive word group) ———————————————————————— ————————————————————————. Note to student: You are now ready for Unit Test 7. 1525

Hurray!
A home run!
 	
1711
	Sentences that have the form of questions, commands, and requests can be punctuated with exclamation points if they show strong feeling.
	
	    a. **The cake is burning!**
	    b. **Don't sit on the baby!**
	
	Which sentence has the form of a command? ____ 1712

No, him. 1898	**However Fritzie frequently whined and cried and howled** 1899
	Do you remember how to place apostrophes in nouns to show ownership? Ask yourself the question "Whom (*or* What) does it belong to?" Then put the apostrophe right after the word that answers this question. **my** *cousins* **house** If the answer is *cousin*, put the apostrophe after the (*n, s*). 2086

motor 23	A noun is a word used to name a *person, place, thing,* or an _____. 24
red 211	*short* **pencil**　　*thin* **pencil**　　*blue* **pencil**　　*soft* **pencil** Each of these pairs of words gives you a different picture. The word that changes each picture is the (*first, second*) word of each pair. 212
b 399	**a. My friend came** *over* **the new road.** **b. My friend came** *over* **recently.** In which sentence is *over* used as a preposition? ____ 400
taken 587	Write the two past forms of **take:** I _____ **my test after Helen** *had* _____ **hers.** 588
plural 775	Underline two plural nouns: **box**　　**shoes**　　**pen**　　**house**　　**streets** 776
b 963	A few short adverbs can be used either with or without *–ly* to describe the action of a verb. **slow** *or* **slowly**　　　**loud** *or* **loudly**　　　**fair** *or* **fairly** **quick** *or* **quickly**　　**plain** *or* **plainly**　　**cheap** *or* **cheaply** **a. He talks too** *loud.*　　**b. He talks too** *loudly.* Are both the above sentences correct? (*Yes, No*) 964

1151

She, I

1151

Now let's "split the doubles" in the sentence below:

Dad took (he, him) and (I, me) to the Dog Show.

SPLIT: Dad took *him* . . . .   Dad took *me* . . . .
Now underline the same pronouns in the combined sentence:

Dad took (*he, him*) and (*I, me*) to the Dog Show.

1152

Whenever (When, As, While) Mike plays the trombone,

1338

The grocer tries to please us. *We are steady customers.*

The grocer tries to please us _____

_____ .

1339

Rip Van Winkle, the main character, slept for twenty years.

1525

UNIT 8: AVOIDING SENTENCE FRAGMENTS AND RUN–ONS

Lesson **53** No Fragments, Please!

[Frames 1527-1554]

---

b

1712

---

a. **Why do you say such things!**
b. **The milk is boiling over!**

Which sentence has the form of a question? _____

1713

However, howled.

1899

Would a dog howl like this if he were not being mistreated

1900

---

n

2086

---

my *cousins* **house**

If the answer is *cousins,* put the apostrophe after the (*n, s*).

2087

page 48

idea	In grammar, a word that is used to name a *person*, *place*, *thing*, or an *idea* is called a _____.
24	25

first	*thin* **pencil**
	In grammar, we say that the word *thin* modifies the noun **pencil**. In everyday language *to modify* means "to change."
	To *modify* your plans means to _____ your plans in some way.
212	213

a	a. **Virginia had never flown** *before*.
	b. **Virginia had never flown** *before* **this trip.**
	In which sentence is *before* used as an adverb? ___
400	401

took, taken	Underline the correct form of the verb:
	Someone must have (*took*, *taken*) **the wrong coat.**
588	589

shoes, streets	When we want to know whether a word is singular or plural, we ask, "What is its *number*?"
	door window floor wall
	All these nouns are singular in _____.
776	777

Yes	a. **The bus goes** *slowly*.
	b. **The bus stops too** *frequently*.
	In which sentence would it be all right to drop the *–ly* from the italicized adverb? ___
964	965

him, me 1152	**Bob was looking for (he, him) and (she, her).** SPLIT: Bob was looking for *him*. Bob was looking for *her*. Underline the correct pronouns: **Bob was looking for** (*he, him*) **and** (*she, her*). 1153
because (since, as) we are steady customers. 1339	*You rotate the tires.* **They will last longer.** _____, **they will last longer.** 1340
	Ordinarily, we should write our thoughts in complete sentences, not in parts of sentences. **We went to a lake for two weeks.** This is a complete sentence with both a subject and a _____. 1527
a 1713	a. **Who cares what he does?** b. **Who cares what he does!** Both sentences are worded like questions. Which shows stronger feeling? ____ 1714
mistreated? 1900	**When the Hunters heard this accusation they were of course quite puzzled** 1901
s 2087	**One** *girls* **picture was in the paper.** The picture belongs to one *girl*. Therefore, we write (*girl's, girls'*). 2088

Lesson 2 Pronouns Come In Handy

[Frames 27-56]

change

If the design of a car is *modified,* is the car the same as it was before? (*Yes, No*)

213   214

a

A noun or pronoun that completes the meaning of a preposition is called its (*subject, object*).

401   402

taken

a. **Someone** *had* **. . . my keys.**
b. **Someone . . . my keys.**

In which sentence would *took* be the correct verb? ____

589   590

number

Suppose that we have three chairs for five people, or five chairs for three people. Do the chairs and the people agree in number? (*Yes, No*)

777   778

a

In this and the following frames, underline the correct modifier. Be sure to choose the adverb (*–ly*) form when the word describes the action of the verb.

This paint dries more (*rapid, rapidly*).

965   966

him, her 1153	**Mr. Roth thanked (he, him) and (I, me) for our help.** Underline the correct pronouns in the "split" sentences: **Mr. Roth thanked** (*he, him*) **for our help. Mr. Roth thanked** (*I, me*) **for our help.** 1154
If (When, After, Because) you rotate the tires, 1340	**The meeting will be held at night.** *Parents can attend it.* **The meeting will be held at night** _____ _____ . 1341
verb 1527	A branch broken off a tree is not a tree. It is only a piece of a tree. In the same way, a piece broken off a sentence is not a complete sentence. It is only a piece of a sentence. a. **We went to a lake for two weeks.** b. **We went to a lake. For two weeks.** In which line do you find a piece of a sentence? ____ 1528
b 1714	a. **Keep off the street!** b. **Keep off the street.** Both sentences are worded like commands. Which shows stronger feeling? ____ 1715
accusation, were, course, puzzled. 1901	**What an embarrassing situation** 1902
girl's 2088	**These** *girls* **picture was in the paper.** The picture belongs to several *girls*. Therefore, we write (*girl's, girls'*). 2089

We have just studied the kind of word that names the persons, places, things, and ideas we talk about.

These name words are called _____.

27

No

214

blue **pencil**   thin **pencil**

When we say that the words *blue* and *thin* modify the noun **pencil,** we mean that they _____ our picture of the pencil.

215

---

object

402

A group of words that starts with a preposition and ends with its object is called a *prepositional* _____.

403

---

b

590

PRESENT   SIMPLE PAST   PAST WITH HELPER
   eat   **ate**   **(have) eaten**

We say, "Virginia *ate* her lunch," but we say, "Virginia *has* _____ her lunch."

591

No

778

Now suppose that we have three chairs for three people. Do the chairs and the people agree in number? (*Yes, No*)

779

---

rapidly

966

The tailor mended the hole very (*skillful, skillfully*).

967

him, me

1154

Underline the correct pronouns:

Mr. Roth thanked (*he, him*) **and** (*I, me*) **for our help.**

1155

---

so that parents
can attend it.

1341

I never met my grandmother. **I feel that I know her.**

_____,

I feel that I know her. (Try the clause signal *Although*.)

1342

---

b

1528

We went to a lake. *For two weeks.*

The italicized word group has been cut off from the sentence by a period and a capital letter.

For two weeks.

Does this cut-off word group have both a subject and a verb? (*Yes, No*)

1529

---

a

1715

In this and in each of the following frames, supply two end marks:

We have chocolate and vanilla_____ Which do you prefer_____

1716

---

situation!

1902

They loved Fritzie took good care of him and never beat him

1903

---

girls'

2089

The *childrens* **room has many books.**

The room belongs to the *children*.
Therefore, we write (*children's, childrens'*).

2090

nouns

27

Pete **felt** *Pete's* **pocket to see if** *Pete* **had** *Pete's* **wallet with** *Pete*.

This sentence sounds foolish because there are five nouns that all refer to _____.

28

---

change

215

path   *narrow* **path**

Adding the word *narrow* to the noun **path** makes your picture of the path (*more, less*) clear.

216

---

phrase

403

∘ Lesson **14** **Prepositional Phrases Can Modify**

[Frames 405-437]

---

eaten

591

Write the two past forms of **eat:**

I _____ **only one piece of pie, but I could** *have* _____ **several pieces.**

592

Yes

779

A subject and a verb must agree in number, too—just like the chairs and the people.

If the subject is singular, the verb must be singular. If the subject is plural, the verb must be plural.

If we use a plural verb with a singular subject, do the subject and verb agree in number? (*Yes, No*)

780

---

skillfully

967

My friends were quite (*curious, curiously*) **about my grades.**

968

page 55

him, me 1155	**Ruth had a message for (she, her) and (I, me).** Underline the correct pronouns in the "split" sentences: **Ruth had a message for** (*she, her*). **Ruth had a message for** (*I, me*). 1156
Although (Though) I never met my grandmother, 1342	**I didn't know the time.** *My watch had stopped.* **I didn't know the time** _____ _____. 1343
No 1529	*For two weeks.* Does this cut-off word group express a complete thought? (*Yes, No*) _____ 1530
vanilla. prefer? 1716	**Have you seen their new car____ It's a total wreck____** 1717
Fritzie, him, him. 1903	**What was the cause of the howling** 1904
children's 2090	In this and the following frames, place the apostrophe correctly in each italicized word: **Louis got only one** *persons* **opinion.** 2091

Pete 28	*his* *he* *his* *Pete* **felt** ~~*Pete's*~~ **pocket to see if** ~~*Pete*~~ **had** ~~*Pete's*~~ **wallet with** *him* ~~*Pete.*~~ Now the sentence is better because we use the noun *Pete* only _____. (How many times?) 29
more 216	A word that is used to modify a noun or pronoun is called an **adjective**. **The** *loud* **noise awoke us.** Because it modifies the noun **noise,** the word *loud* is an _____. 217
	Most prepositional phrases are used like adjectives and adverbs to modify other words. a. **a** *cream* **pitcher** b. **a pitcher** *for cream* Both the adjective *cream* in *a* and the prepositional phrase *for cream* in *b* modify the noun _____. 405
ate, eaten 592	Underline the correct form of the verb: **Jimmy** *has* (*eaten, ate*) **all his salad.** 593
No 780	Most plural nouns end in **s** (*dogs, cars, books*) or **es** (*boxes, dishes, churches*). However, a small number of plural nouns do not end in **s** or **es**. Underline three plural nouns: **farm men children boy teeth school** 781
curious 968	**It rains rather** (*regular, regularly*) **during November.** 969

her, me 1156	Underline the correct pronouns: **Ruth had a message for** (*she, her*) **and** (*I, me*). 1157
because (since, as) my watch had stopped. 1343	*I was about to receive the medal.* **I suddenly awoke from my dream.** _____, **I suddenly awoke from my dream.** 1344

No
 	
 1530
	To be a complete sentence, a group of words must pass two tests:
	     1. It must have both a subject and a verb.
	     2. It must express a complete thought.
	
	        For two weeks.
	
	 Does this word group pass either test? (*Yes, No*) 1531

car? wreck! (*or* wreck.) 1717	**Gosh_____ What awful weather_____** 1718
howling? 1904	**Fritzie was very sensitive and a scolding would make him cry** 1905
person's 2091	**There are several** *doctors* **offices in this building.** 2092

once (one time) 29	*his* *he* *his* Pete felt ~~Pete's~~ pocket to see if ~~Pete~~ had ~~Pete's~~ wallet with *him* ~~Pete~~. The words that we put in place of the nouns *Pete* and *Pete's* are called **pronouns**. A *pronoun* is a word used in place of a _____. 30
adjective 217	**After looking at the balloons, the child chose a *red* one.** The word *red* is an adjective because it modifies the pronoun _____. 218
pitcher 405	a. **a *cream* pitcher** b. **A pitcher *for cream*** Both the word *cream* in *a* and the prepositional phrase *for cream* in *b* are used as (*adjectives, adverbs*). 406
eaten 593	a. **The boys ... all the cookies.** b. **The boys *have* ... all the cookies.** In which sentence would *ate* be the correct verb? ____ 594
men, children, teeth 781	PLURAL: <u>Bees sting.</u> In this plural sentence, there is an **s** at the end of the (*subject, verb*). 782
regularly 969	**You can live very (*comfortable, comfortably*) in one of these cabins.** 970

her, me 1157	Instead of two pronouns, our pair sometimes consists of a noun and a pronoun. Just drop the noun, and try the pronoun by itself. This will tell you which pronoun to use. **Don will call for ~~Karen and~~ (I, me).** Underline the correct pronoun: NOUN DROPPED: **Don will call for (I, me).** 1158
As (When) I was about to receive the medal, 1344	*We bought a car.* **We first tried out several makes.** _____, **we first tried out several makes.** 1345
No 1531	A *fragment* means a piece of something that has been cut off or broken off—like a fragment of wood or glass. A word or word group that has been broken off from a sentence is a **sentence fragment**. It is a bad mistake in writing. Underline the sentence fragment: **We went to a lake. For two weeks.** 1532
Gosh! weather! 1718	**First, boil the milk____ Have you done that yet____** 1719
sensitive, cry. 1905	**The slightest push tap or shove would make him howl** 1906
doctors' 2092	**The car spattered both *womens* dresses.** 2093

noun 30	By using pronouns in place of nouns, we avoid (*repetition, discourtesy*). 31
one 218	Underline two adjectives in this sentence: **Old people usually enjoy young children.** 219
adjectives 406	a. *winter* **clothing** b. **clothing** *for winter* The prepositional phrase *for winter* in *b* does the same job as the adjective _____ in *a*. 407
a 594	PRESENT SIMPLE PAST PAST WITH HELPER **fall** **fell** **(have) fallen** We say, "The picture *fell* down," but we say, "The picture *has* _____ down." 595
subject 782	SINGULAR: **A <u>bee</u> <u>stings</u>.** In this singular sentence, there is an **s** at the end of the (*subject, verb*). 783
comfortably 970	**The pitch was as (*swift, swiftly*) as a bullet.** 971

me

1158

Underline the correct pronoun:

Don will call for Karen and (*I*, *me*).

1159

Before we
bought a car,

1345

A bee stung me. *I was mowing the lawn.*

A bee stung me _____

_____.

1346

For two weeks.

1532

We went to a lake. *For two weeks.*

For two weeks is a prepositional phrase that modifies the
verb **went**.

Should a prepositional phrase be cut off from the word
that it modifies? (*Yes, No*)

1533

---

milk. yet?

1719

Do you expect to see Don____ I have a message for him____

1720

---

push, tap,
howl.

1906

**If Mr. or Mrs. Hunter spoke loudly to the dog he would cry
mournfully**

1907

---

women's

2093

All the *boys* **faces needed washing.**

2094

repetition 31	a. **George read the** *story*. b. **George read** *it*. Is the italicized word a pronoun in sentence *a* or *b*? _____ 32
Old, young 219	The little words **a, an,** and **the** are a special kind of adjective. Don't include them when you pick out adjectives in this lesson. Underline two adjectives in this sentence: **The yellow tulips are a beautiful sight.** 220
winter 407	A prepositional phrase can also do the job of an adverb by describing the action of a verb. a. **drove** *cautiously* b. **drove** *with caution* Both the adverb *cautiously* in *a* and the prepositional phrase *with caution* in *b* modify the verb _____. 408
fallen 595	Write the two past forms of **fall:** **The picture** _____ **just after I** *had* _____ **asleep.** 596
verb 783	PLURAL: **Bees sting.** SINGULAR: **A bee stings.** Adding an **s** to the noun **Bee** makes it plural. Does adding an **s** to the verb **sting** make it plural? (*Yes, No*) 784
swift 971	**The fire engines came so** (*prompt, promptly*) **that little damage was done.** 972

me	The ~~Barts and~~ (we, us) attend the same church. Underline the correct pronoun: NOUN DROPPED: (*We, Us*) attend the same church.
1159	1160

while (as, when) I was mowing the lawn.	Lesson **46** Meet the Adjective Clause [Frames 1348-1376]
1346	

No	Underline the prepositional phrase that is written as a sentence fragment: Betty wrote a story. About a lost dog.
1533	1534

Don? him.	Stop___ Don't you hear that train whistle___
1720	1721

dog, mournfully.	Yes the Hunters sometimes scolded their dog but they never beat him
1907	1908

boys'	*Childrens* meals should include milk.
2094	2095

b

32

a. **George read the** *story.*
b. **George read** *it.*

The pronoun *it* in sentence *b* takes the place of the noun

_____ in sentence *a.*

33

---

yellow, beautiful

220

Some words can be used as either pronouns or adjectives.

a. **Rex ate both.**
b. **Rex ate both sandwiches.**

In which sentence is **both** used as an adjective? _____

221

---

drove

408

a. **drove** *cautiously*
b. **drove** *with caution*

Both the word *cautiously* in *a* and the prepositional phrase *with caution* in *b* are used as (*adjectives, adverbs*).

409

---

fell, fallen

596

Underline the correct form of the verb:

The leaves *have* (*fallen, fell*) **from the trees.**

597

No

784

Although adding an **s** to a noun always makes it plural, adding an **s** to a verb makes it _____.

785

---

promptly

972

Claire didn't seem (*happy, happily*) **about her invitation.**

973

We 1160	Underline the correct pronoun: **The Barts and (*we, us*) attend the same church.** 1161
	All the clauses in the previous two lessons explained *when, where, how, why* or *on what condition* the action of the sentence took place. Because these clauses do the job of adverbs, we call them _____ clauses. 1348
About a lost dog. 1534	Underline the prepositional phrases that are written as a sentence fragment: **I recognized my dog. By the spot on its ear.** 1535
Stop! whistle? (*or* whistle!) 1721	Lesson **60** Periods for Abbreviations [Frames 1723-1745]
Yes, dog, him. 1908	**As Mr. Hunter was talking to the policemen Fritzie came to investigate** 1909
Children's 2095	In this and the following frames, write between the parentheses the correct contraction for each pair of italicized words. *They are* (_____) **sure that** *you are* (_____) **not going.** 2096

story 33	a. **I took** *her* **picture.** b. **I took** *Nancy's* **picture.** Is the italicized word a pronoun in sentence *a* or *b*? ____ 34
b 221	a. *short* **pencil** *thin* **pencil** *blue* **pencil** *soft* **pencil** b. *this* **pencil** *that* **pencil** *two* **pencils** *some* **pencils** In which group do the italicized adjectives answer the question *What kind?* ____ 222
adverbs 409	a. **replied** *angrily* b. **replied** *with anger* The prepositional phrase *with anger* in *b* does the same job as the adverb _____ in *a*. 410
fallen 597	a. **The child** *had* ... **into the bathtub.** b. **The child** ... **into the bathtub.** In which sentence would *fell* be the correct word? ____ 598
singular 785	We say, "The window<u>s</u> open," but we say, "The window open<u>s</u>." We say, "The mountain<u>s</u> rise," but we say, "The mountain _____." 786
happy 973	Lesson **33** **Using** *Good* **and** *Well* **Correctly** *page 67* [Frames 975-995]

we 1161	In this and the following frames, underline the correct pronoun or pronouns. Remember to use the same pronouns in pairs that you would use singly: **Miss Roberts put** (*he, him*) **and** (*I, me*) **at the same desk.** 1162
adverb 1348	In this lesson we study clauses that do the job of adjectives. First, let us look at any ordinary adjective: **We need an** *energetic* **salesman.** The word *energetic* is an adjective because it modifies the noun _____. 1349
By the spot on its ear. 1535	Sometimes a sentence fragment is cut off from the beginning of a sentence: a. **From my bedroom window. I can see the park.** b. **I can see the park. From my bedroom window.** In which line does the sentence fragment come first? _____ 1536
	Put a period after every abbreviated word. With a few exceptions, abbreviations should be avoided in ordinary writing. Here are some abbreviations that it is correct to use: **Mr. and Mrs. (But Miss takes no period!)** Supply the missing periods: **Miss Brooks is the guest of Mr and Mrs Lasky.** 1723
policemen, investigate. 1909	**Fritzie playfully jumped on one of the policemen and Mr. Hunter pushed the dog back** 1910
They're, you're 2096	*Let us* (_____) **see if** *he will* (_____) **lend us his boat.** 2097

a

a. **I took** *her* **picture.**
b. **I took** *Nancy's* **picture.**

The pronoun *her* in sentence *a* takes the place of the noun

_____ in sentence *b*.

34

35

---

a

Here are other questions that adjectives can answer about nouns.

Which one(s)?   *How many?*   *How much?*

I like *these* **shoes.**

The adjective *these* answers the question "_____?"

222

223

---

angrily

a. **We ate** *under the tree.*
b. **The ground** *under the tree* **was dry.**

In which sentence does the prepositional phrase modify

the verb? ____

410

411

---

b

(have) driven   (have) spoken   (have) taken   (have) fallen
(have) broken   (have) written   (have) eaten

The helper form of every verb in this lesson ends with the

two letters _____.

598

599

---

rises

We say, "The vegetables grow," but we say, "The vegetable

_____."

786

787

The word **good** is an adjective. Like any other adjective, it can modify only a noun or a pronoun.

The road was *good.*

The adjective *good* modifies the noun _____.

975

him, me 1162	(*He, him*) **and** (*I, me*) **were waiting for a bus.** 1163
salesman 1349	a. **We need an** *energetic* **salesman.** b. **We need a salesman** *who is energetic.* The clause *who is energetic* in sentence *b* does the same job that the adjective _____ does in sentence *a*. 1350
a 1536	a. **From my bedroom window. I can see the park.** b. **From my bedroom window I can see the park.** c. **I can see the park. From my bedroom window.** Which arrangement is correct? ____ 1537

Mr.   Mrs.
 	
1723
	Here are other correct abbreviations:
	
	    T. N. Stevens (after initials in names)
	    Dr. Meyers (only when used with a name)
	
	Supply the missing periods:
	
	    Dr Nolan is a cousin of C N Jackson.
	
	1724

policemen, back. 1910	**Mr. Hunter gave Fritzie only a slight shove but the dog yelped loudly** (Are there both a subject and a verb after the conjunction *but?*) 1911
Let's, he'll 2097	*There is* (_____) **a car that** *I would* (_____) **like to drive.** 2098

Nancy's 35	a. **The** *milk* **is sour.** b. *This* **is sour.** Is the italicized word a pronoun in sentence *a* or *b*? ____ 36
"Which ones?" 223	a. **The club has** *little* **money.** b. **I belong to** *three* **clubs.** c. **I joined** *that* **club.** In which sentence does the adjective answer the question *How many?* ____ 224

a
 	
411
	A prepositional phrase that is used as an adverb is called an **adverb phrase.**
	
	    a. **We ate** *under the tree.*
	    b. **The ground** *under the tree* **was dry.**
	
	In which sentence is the prepositional phrase an *adverb* phrase because it modifies the verb? ____
	
	412

–en 599	a. **driven spoken taken fallen broken written eaten** b. **drove spoke took fell broke wrote ate** Which group of verb forms should be used after the helping verb **have, has,** or **had?** ____ 600
grows 787	Al! the verbs in this lesson show *present* time. The problem of subject-verb agreement does not arise when we use *simple past* verbs (except for the verb **be**). SIMPLE PAST: **The boy laughed.** If you changed the subject **boy** to **boys,** would you need to change the verb **laughed?** (*Yes, No*) 788
road 975	Can an adjective tell *how* about the action of a verb? (*Yes, No*) 976

He, I 1163	**Were you able to get tickets for Peggy and** (*I, me*)**?** 1164
energetic 1350	**We need a salesman** *who is energetic.* Because the clause *who is energetic* modifies the noun **salesman,** it is an _____ clause. 1351

b
 	
 1537
	Here again are the two tests for a complete sentence:
	     1. It must have both a subject and a verb.
	     2. It must express a complete thought.
	       A <u>bowl</u> of fruit <u>stood</u> on the table.
	 Has this word group a subject and a verb? (*Yes, No*)
	
	 1538

Dr.   C. N.
 	
 1724
	These abbreviations are customary in stating times of the
	 day:
	         8:00 A.M. **6:30** P.M.
	 Supply the missing periods:
	     The zoo is open from 10:00 A M **to 5:30** P M
	
	 1725

shove, loudly. 1911	**The policemen laughed and went on their way** 1912
There's, I'd 2098	**Miss Baxter** *does not* (_____) **think that** *you have* (_____) **read the story.** 2099

b 36	a. **The** *milk* **is sour.** b. *This* **is sour.** The pronoun *This* in sentence *b* takes the place of the noun _____ in sentence *a*. 37
b 224	a. **The club has** *little* **money.** b. **I belong to** *three* **clubs.** c. **I joined** *that* **club.** In which sentence does the adjective answer the question *Which one?* ____ 225
a 412	A prepositional phrase that is used as an adjective is called an **adjective phrase.** a. **I went** *to the basement* **for some tools.** b. **The stairs** *to the basement* **were slippery.** In which sentence is the prepositional phrase an *adjective* phrase because it modifies a noun? ____ 413
a 600	Write the correct past form of each verb in parentheses: **Mr. Phillips had** _____ (*speak*) **to George about the excuse he had** _____ (*write*). 601
No 788	Adding an **s** to a verb that shows present time always makes it singular. However, a verb without an **s** can be either singular or plural, depending upon the subject. SINGULAR: *I* **want.** *He* **wants.** *She* **wants.** *It* **wants.** Do all the singular verbs end in **s**? (*Yes, No*) 789
No 976	WRONG: **This radio plays** *good.* This sentence is wrong because the adjective *good* cannot be used to tell *how* the radio _____. 977

me 1164	(*She, Her*) and (*I, me*) tried out for the school play. 1165
adjective 1351	Here is the adjective clause by itself: *who is energetic* What is the subject of the verb *is*? _____ 1352
Yes 1538	**A bowl of fruit stood on the table.** Does this word group express a complete thought? (*Yes, No*) 1539
A.M. P.M. 1725	Use abbreviations to state historical dates: **1000 B.C.** (for Before Christ) **A.D. 732** (for the Latin phrase Anno Domini, meaning "in the year of our Lord") **The period from 50 B C to A D 116 is known as the "Golden Age" of Latin literature.** 1726
way. 1912	**Well have you ever heard of a dog as sensitive as Fritzie** Note to student: You are now ready for Unit Test 9. 1913
doesn't, you've 2099	In this and the following frames, underline the correct word in each pair: **Why don't you borrow (*her's, hers*)?** 2100

milk

37

---

a. *Some* **were hungry.**
b. **The** *children* **were hungry.**

Is the italicized word a pronoun in sentence *a* or *b*? ____

38

---

c

225

---

a. **The club has** *little* **money.**
b. **I belong to** *three* **clubs.**
c. **I joined** *that* **club.**

In which sentence does the adjective answer the question

How much? ____

226

---

b

413

Now let's think, for a moment, about ordinary adverbs.

A bus *finally* **came along.**

The adverb *finally* modifies the verb _____.

414

---

spoken, written

601

Write the correct past form of each verb in parentheses:

The cows have _____ (*eat***) the apples that have**

_____ (*fall***) to the ground.**

602

No

789

Although we use the pronoun **you** in speaking to one person or to many, it always requires a plural verb.

SINGULAR: <u>You</u> (one person) <u>live near me.</u>
PLURAL: <u>You</u> (several persons) <u>live near me.</u>

In both sentences, we use the plural verb _____.

790

---

plays

977

An adjective cannot modify a verb.

To modify a verb, we need to use an _____.

978

She, I	We didn't know whether the car had stopped for Peggy or (*I, me*).
1165	1166

who	**We need a salesman** *who is energetic.* The clause signal that starts the adjective clause in this sentence is _____.
1352	1353

Yes	Now we shall split the sentence in two: WRONG: **A <u>bowl</u> of fruit. <u>Stood</u> on the table.** Does either word group have both a subject and a verb? (*Yes, No*)
1539	1540

B.C. A.D.	In abbreviating the names of well-known organizations, you may either use periods or omit them.
	
	    P.T.A. *or* **PTA** (Parent-Teacher Association)
	    R.O.T.C. *or* **ROTC** (Reserve Officers' Training Corps)
	
	 Supply the missing periods:
	
	    We meet at 8:00 P M at the Y M C A every Monday.

1726	1727

Well, Fritzie?	UNIT 10: **APOSTROPHES AND QUOTATION MARKS** Lesson **67** Apostrophes for Showing Ownership [Frames 1915-1948]
1913	

hers	(*Theirs, Their's*) **is an Irish terrier.**
2100	2101

a

a. **Kip and Dennis were absent from school.**
b. *Both* **were absent from school.**

How many nouns in sentence *a* does the word *Both* in sentence *b* take the place of? _____

38   39

---

a

I enjoy . . . movies.

Underline the adjective that could be used in the above sentence to answer the question *What kind?*

most   those   Western   few

226   227

---

came

Finally **a bus came along.**
A bus *finally* **came along.**
A bus came along *finally.*

Is the adverb *finally* always next to the word **came**, which it modifies? (*Yes, No*)

414   415

---

eaten, fallen

Write the correct past form of each verb in parentheses:

Chester has _____ (*take*) **the letter that he has**
_____ (*write*) **to the mailbox.**

602   603

---

live

When both the subject and the verb are singular, or when both the subject and the verb are plural, we say that they agree in number.

    a. **His brothers own the garage.**
    b. **His brothers owns the garage.**

In which sentence do the subject and verb agree? ____

790   791

---

adverb

The word **well** can be used as an adverb to describe the action of a verb.

    RIGHT: **This radio plays** *well.*

This sentence is right because we use the adverb _____ to tell *how* the radio **plays.**

978   979

me 1166	Will Uncle Steve take (*she, her*) **and** (*I, me*) **to the fair?** 1167
who 1353	**We need a salesman** *who is energetic.* The clause signal *who* is a pronoun because it refers to the noun _____. 1354
No 1540	**A <u>bowl</u> of fruit. <u>Stood</u> on the table.** Does either of these word groups express a complete thought? (*Yes, No*) 1541
P.M. Y.M.C.A. (*or* YMCA) 1727	In lists and schedules where the same words are repeated, certain abbreviations may be used to save space. ADDRESSES: **St.** (Street) **Rd.** (Road) **Rte.** (Route) **Ave.** (Avenue) **Blvd.** (Boulevard) **Bldg.** (Building) Is it proper to use these abbreviations in ordinary writing? (*Yes, No*) 1728
	There are two different ways of showing ownership or belonging: a. **The room of Robert** b. **Robert's room** Both of the above examples show that the **room** belongs to _____. 1915
Theirs 2101	**You left** (*your's, yours*) **in your locker.** 2102

two 39	*Both* **were absent from school.** The word *Both* is a _____. 40
Western 227	**We bought . . . tires.** Underline the adjective that could be used in the above sentence to answer the question *How many?* **several new those expensive** 228
No 415	*After several minutes,* **a bus came along.** The adverb phrase *after several minutes* modifies the verb **came** because it tells (*when, where, how*) the bus **came.** 416
taken, written 603	Write the correct past form of each verb in parentheses: **The man had** _____ (*drive*) **into a tree and had** _____ (*break*) **the bumper.** 604
a 791	Now let's look at a compound subject that has two parts: <u>John</u> *and* <u>Steve</u> <u>own</u> **the garage.** How many persons own the garage? _____ 792
well 979	a. **This radio plays** *good.* b. **This radio plays** *well.* Which sentence is correct? ____ 980

her, me 1167	The Wilsons and (*we, us*) shared the cost of the fence. 1168
salesman 1354	Let's try another sentence: The road *that we took* was shorter. The clause *that we took* modifies the noun _____. 1355
No 1541	A <u>bowl</u> of fruit. <u>Stood</u> on the table. How many sentence fragments do we have here? _____ 1542
No 1728	These abbreviations may be used for lists and schedules: GEOGRAPHICAL **N.Y.** (New York) **Ft. Dodge** (Fort) NAMES: **Wis.** (Wisconsin) **Mt. Vernon** (Mount) **Tenn.** (Tennessee) **Highland Pk.** (Park) Supply the missing periods: **Chairman: F S Stocker, Ft Wayne, Ind** 1729
Robert 1915	a. **the room of Robert** b. **Robert's room** In example *a*, we show ownership by using an *of* phrase. In example *b*, we show ownership by adding ____ to the noun **Robert**. 1916
yours 2102	(*Its, It's*) **afraid of** (*its, it's*) **own shadow.** 2103

pronoun	**Most people like them.**
	The pronoun in this sentence is the word _____.
40	41

several	**We filled the jar with ... water.**
	Underline the adjective that could be used in the above sentence to answer the question *How much?*
	fresh some this salt
228	229

when	*After several minutes,* **a bus came along.**
	How many words stand between the adverb phrase and the verb **came,** which it modifies? _____
416	417

driven, broken	Lesson **20** **Six More Irregular Verbs**
604	[Frames 606-634]

two	**John** *and* **Steve own the garage.**
	Because two persons own the garage, the subject of the verb **own** is (*singular, plural*).
792	793

b	Always use the adverb **well,** not the adjective **good,** to tell *how* about the action of a verb.
	a. **These scissors cut well.**
	b. **These scissors are good.**
	In which sentences does the verb show action? ____
980	981

we 1168	**Neither the Roses nor** (*they, them*) **had heard the news.** 1169
road 1355	**The road** *that we took* **was shorter.** Because the clause *that we took* modifies the noun _____, it is an _____ clause. 1356

two
 	
1542
	Tests for a sentence:
	    1. It must have both a subject and a verb.
	    2. It must express a complete thought.
	If a group of words fails either one of these tests, it is not
	a sentence, but a sentence _____.
	1543

F. S.   Ft.
Ind.
 	
1729
	Days of the week and months of the year may be abbreviated on lists and schedules, too, to save space.
	    DAYS: **Sat.** (Saturday) **Wed.** (Wednesday)
	    MONTHS: **Feb.** (February) **Dec.** (December)
	Supply the missing periods:
	    Track meet: 4:00 P M , Fri , Oct 21.
	1730

's 1916	To show ownership, we often put two nouns in a row. The first noun, with the apostrophe, shows the owner. The second noun, without the apostrophe, shows what is owned. **boy's bicycle man's job dog's tail** In each of these examples, the owner is shown by the (*first, second*) word. 1917
It's, its 2103	(*Whose, Who's*) **the boy** (*whose, who's*) **model plane won?** 2104

them	**Most people like** *them.*
	Do you know whether the pronoun *them* refers to dogs, biscuits, or movies? *(Yes, No)*
41	42

some	In this and the following frames, underline three adjectives in each sentence. Omit the special adjectives *a, an,* and *the.*
	Castles were cold, damp, and dark places.
229	230

two	If a phrase answers a question like *When? Where?* or *How?* about the verb, it is an adverb phrase—wherever it may come.
	We reached the fruit *with a ladder.*
	The adverb phrase *with a ladder* modifies **reached** because it tells *(when, where, how)* we **reached** the fruit.
417	418

	Look at the simple past forms of these four verbs. Notice how similar they are:
	SIMPLE PAST: **flew grew knew threw**
	Do any of these simple past forms end in *–ed?* (*Yes, No*)
	606

plural	**John** *and* **Steve own the garage.**
	Two singular subjects connected by the conjunction *and* require a *(singular, plural)* verb.
793	794

a	**These scissors cut (good, well).**
	The verb **cut** is an action verb. Therefore, to tell *how* the scissors **cut**, we would use the adverb _____.
981	982

they 1169	Dad settled the argument between my brother and (*I, me*). 1170
road, adjective 1356	Here is the adjective clause by itself: *that <u>we</u> <u>took</u>* The subject of the verb *took* is _____. 1357
fragment 1543	In this and the following frames, you will find two word groups. One of them is a correct sentence; the other is incorrect because it is a sentence fragment. In the blank space, write the letter of the complete sentence. a. **The driver of the other car.** b. **My friend drove the other car.** _____ 1544
P.M. Fri. Oct. 1730	Abbreviate titles only when used with names: TITLES: **Gov. Burns** (Governor) **Fr. Bradley** (Father) **Pres. Taft** (President) **Sr. Mary Agnes** (Sister) **Prof. White** (Professor) **Rev. Paul Smith** (Reverend) Supply the missing periods: **Committee: Prof Stone, Supt Curtis, Fr Brown, Dr Krohn** 1731
first 1917	a. **one** *boy's* **locker** b. **several** *boys'* **lockers** Look at the noun with an apostrophe in each example. Does the apostrophe come before the *s* in each example? (*Yes, No*) 1918
Who's, whose 2104	(*Your, You're*) **friend knows that** (*your, you're*) **sorry.** 2105

No 42	a. **Most people like** *dogs*. b. **Most people like** *them*. One of these sentences is more definite than the other. The more definite sentence is the one with the italicized *(noun, pronoun)*. 43
cold, damp, dark 230	Underline three adjectives: **The little kitten has long, sharp claws.** 231
how 418	**We reached the fruit** *with a ladder.* How many words stand between the adverb phrase and the verb it modifies? _____ 419
No 606	SIMPLE PAST: **flew grew knew threw** Write the simple past form of each verb in parentheses: **Chuck** _____ *(grow)* **impatient with the puzzle and** _____ *(throw)* **it aside.** 607
plural 794	Now let's change the conjunction *and* to *or*: <u>John</u> *or* <u>Steve</u> <u>owns</u> **the garage.** The above sentence is another way of saying **John owns the garage, or Steve** _____ **the garage.** 795
well 982	Underline the correct modifier: **This pen writes** *(well, good).* 983

Lesson **40** Supplying the Missing Words

[Frames 1172-1200]

---

we

1357

The road *that we took* **was shorter.**

The clause signal that starts the adjective clause in this sentence is _____.

1358

---

b

1544

Continue to write the letter of the complete sentence:

  a. **We won the first game.**
  b. **Won the first game of the season.**

The correct sentence is ____.

1545

Prof.   Supt.
Fr.   Dr.

1731

COMPANIES: **Pacific Power Co.** (Company)
      Briggs Mfg. Co. (Manufacturing Company)
      Robinson Bros. (Brothers)

Supply the missing periods:

  Sponsors: Arrow Oil Co and Proctor Bros of Dayton

1732

No

1918

  a. **one** *boy's* **locker**   b. **several** *boys'* **lockers**

In using apostrophes, the main problem is deciding whether to put the apostrophe before or after the final *s*.

In example *a*, the **locker** belongs to one *boy*.

In example *b*, the **lockers** belong to several _____.

1919

Your, you're

2105

(*Their, They're*) **owner must think that** (*their, they're*) **priceless.**

2106

noun 43	a. *Somebody* **borrowed Sam's pen.** b. *Arthur* **borrowed Sam's pen.** Which sentence is less definite because it contains a pronoun? ____ 44
little, long, sharp 231	Underline three adjectives: **Most blond people have blue eyes.** 232
two 419	**I put the letter** *in the envelope.* The adverb phrase *in the envelope* modifies the verb _____ . 420
grew, threw 607	Write the simple past form of each verb in parentheses: **We** _____ (*know*) **that you** _____ (*fly*) **to Dallas.** 608
owns 795	**John** *or* **Steve owns the garage.** How many persons own the garage? _____ 796
well 983	a. **Our car is . . . .** b. **Our car runs . . . .** In which sentence would it be a mistake to use the adjective **good?** ____ 984

To make comparisons, we often use the words **than** and **as**.

Jerry jumped higher than I jumped.

After the word **than**, we find a second subject and verb.

The pronoun **I** is the subject of the verb _____.

1172

---

that

1358

The road *that we took* **was shorter.**

The clause signal *that* is a pronoun because it refers to the noun _____.

1359

---

a

1545

a. **A trip through a glass factory.**
b. **A trip through a glass factory is interesting.**

The correct sentence is ____.

1546

Co.   Bros.

1732

Do not use an *and* sign (**&**) in place of the word *and* except in notes you might make for *your own* use only.

a. **Please give my regards to your mother & dad.**
b. **Please give my regards to your mother and dad.**

Which sentence would be correct for a personal letter? ____

1733

---

boys

1919

To decide whether to put the apostrophe before or after the final *s* is simple. Ask yourself this question: "Whom does the locker belong to?"

One *boys* locker

In this example, the **locker** belongs to one _____.

1920

Their, they're

2106

After each pair of sentences, write the letter of the sentence that is correctly punctuated and capitalized.

a. **Gordon said "that he slept like a log."**

b. **Gordon said that he slept like a log.** ____

2107

Two of the following words are nouns and two are pro-nouns.

Underline the two pronouns:

these   **magazines**   **boats**   **several**

44

45

Most, blond, blue

Underline three adjectives:

Those handsome wallets cost five dollars.

232

233

---

put

A prepositional phrase that modifies a noun or pronoun is

called an _____ phrase.

420

421

---

knew, flew

Here are the helper forms of these same verbs:

(have) flown   **(have) grown**   **(have) known**   **(have) thrown**

Each of these helper forms ends with the letter ____.

608

609

---

one

John *or* **Steve** **owns the garage.**

Since either **John** or **Steve**—not both—owns the garage,
the subject of the verb **owns** is (*singular, plural*).

796

797

---

b

Our car runs good.

This sentence is wrong because the adjective **good** cannot modify the (*noun, verb*) **runs**.

984

985

jumped 1172	Underline the correct pronoun: **We made more hits than** (*they, them*) **did.** 1173
road 1359	Here are the clause signals that start adjective clauses, There are not very many. ADJECTIVE CLAUSE SIGNALS: **who (whom, whose),** **which, that** Are these words different from the clause signals that start adverb clauses? (*Yes, No*) 1360
b 1546	a. **Suddenly let go of the ladder.** b. **Jeff let go of the ladder.** The correct sentence is ____. 1547
b 1733	a. **Hockey and basketball also interest me.** b. **Hockey & basketball also interest me.** Which sentence would be correct for an English theme? ___ 1734
boy 1920	**one** *boys* **locker** Whom does the **locker** belong to? The answer to this question is *boy*, not *boys*. Therefore, put the apostrophe after *boy*, not after *boys*: **one** *boys* **locker** 1921
b 2107	a. **"Our team is the best," Chuck boasted.** b. **"Our team is the best" Chuck boasted.** ____ 2108

these, several 45	.?. **can swim here.** Underline two pronouns that would fit in the above sentence: **Leroy Anybody Everyone Boys** 46
Those, handsome, five 233	Underline three adjectives: **Several people left the hot, stuffy room.** 234
adjective 421	A prepositional phrase that modifies a verb is called an _____ phrase. 422
–n 609	Write the helper form of each verb in parentheses: **The room** *had* _____(*grow*) **very warm, and I** *had* _____ (*throw*) **off my coat.** 610
singular 797	**John** *or* **Steve owns the garage.** Two singular subjects connected by the conjunction *or* require a (*singular, plural*) verb. 798
verb 985	In this and the following frames, underline two correct modifiers in each sentence. Choose the adjective *good* to modify a noun or pronoun. Choose the adverb *well* to describe the action of a verb. **The food was** (*good, well*), **and we ate** (*good, well*). 986

they 1173	**We made more hits than _they_ did.** We use the subject form of the pronoun because _they_ is the subject of the verb _____. 1174
Yes 1360	ADJECTIVE CLAUSE SIGNALS: **who (whom, whose), which, that** The pronoun **who** has two other forms: _____ and _____. 1361
b 1547	a. **The jet plane had four powerful engines.** b. **A jet plane with four powerful engines.** The correct sentence is ____. 1548
a 1734	In this and the following frames, first put a period after every abbreviation that is proper for ordinary writing. Then, on the blank line, write out in full any word that should not be abbreviated. **The party takes place at 8:00 P M on Fri, Apr 6.** _____ 1735
boy's 1921	**several _boys_ lockers** Whom do the **lockers** belong to? The lockers belong to several _____. 1922
a 2108	a. **The dentist said, "this will hurt for only a minute."** b. **The dentist said, "This will hurt for only a minute."** ____ 2109

Anybody, Everyone 46	*Which* **did you buy?** Do you know whether *Which* refers to a candy bar, a coat, or a car? (*Yes, No*) 47
Several, hot, stuffy 234	Many words can serve as either nouns or adjectives. If the word comes before another noun and tells *what kind*, it is an adjective. a. **The** *morning* **was very cool.** b. **I always read the** *morning* **paper.** The word *morning* is an adjective in sentence ____. 235
adverb 422	Which kind of phrase is more likely to be separated from the word it modifies? An (*adjective, adverb*) phrase. 423
grown, thrown 610	Write the helper form of each verb in parentheses: **The Rosses must** *have* _____ (*know*) **that they could** *have* _____ (*fly*) **there.** 611
singular 798	a. **Frances** *and* **her sister ... with the baby.** b. **Frances** *or* **her sister ... with the baby.** Which sentence requires the singular verb **stays**? ____ 799
good, well 986	**We ate** (*good, well*) **because the food was** (*good, well*). 987

did 1174	Usually we abbreviate (shorten) a comparison by omitting one or more words: **We made more hits than they did.** **We made more hits than they.** We abbreviated this comparison by omitting the verb ____. 1175
whom, whose 1361	ADJECTIVE CLAUSE SIGNALS: **who (whom, whose),** **which, that** Each of these adjective clause signals refers to a noun or another pronoun in the main part of the sentence. These signal words are therefore (*nouns, pronouns*). 1362
a 1548	a. **I planned to study my math before school.** b. **Planning to study my math before school.** The correct sentence is ____. 1549
P.M. Friday, April 1735	**Miss Jansen works for Mr A C Carter of N Y** _____ 1736
boys 1922	**several** *boys* **lockers** This time, the answer to the question "Whom do the **lockers** belong to?" is *boys*, not *boy*. Therefore, put the apostrophe after *boys*, not after *boy*. **several** *boys* **lockers** 1923
b 2109	a. **The man said", This dog doesn't bite".** b. **The man said, "This dog doesn't bite." ____** 2110

No

47

Which **did you buy?**

Because the word *Which* might refer to a great many different things, it is a (*pronoun, noun*).

48

---

b

235

a. **Bob's mother served** *lemon* **pie.**
b. **The** *lemon* **improved the punch.**

The word *lemon* is an adjective in sentence _____.

236

---

adverb

423

Sometimes an adjective phrase seems to answer the question *Where?* about a noun. However, it really modifies the noun by telling *which one*(s) we mean.

The leaves *on this tree* **are falling.**

The prepositional phrase *on this tree* tells which _____ we are talking about.

424

---

known, flown

611

PRESENT	SIMPLE PAST	PAST WITH HELPER
fly	flew	(have) flown
grow	grew	(have) grown
know	knew	(have) known
throw	threw	(have) thrown

Do any of the above verb forms end in *–ed?* (*Yes, No*)

612

---

b

799

a. **The teacher** *or* **a pupil ... the attendance.**
b. **The teacher** *and* **a pupil ... the attendance.**

Which sentence requires the singular verb **takes?** _____

800

---

well, good

987

A person whose health is (*good, well*) **should sleep** (*good, well*).

988

did

1175

We made more hits than *they* did.
We made more hits than *they.*

When we omit the verb **did,** do we still use the same form of the pronoun? (*Yes, No*)

1176

---

pronouns

1362

All the adjective clauses in this lesson start with a clause signal and end when the idea of the clause is completed.

The man *who owns the truck* **lives across the street.**

The adjective clause starts with the clause signal _____

and ends with the word _____.

1363

---

a

1549

---

a. **After the car drove away.**
b. **The car drove away.**

The correct sentence is ____.

1550

Mr. A. C.
New York

1736

The bus runs between Logan St and Evergreen Pk

_____

1737

---

boys'

1923

Place your apostrophe so that the word *before* the apostrophe answers the question "Whom does it belong to?"

boy's   boys'

If the answer to your question is **boy,** which of the above

words would you choose? _____

1924

---

b

2110

---

a. **Roy began, "It was Halloween. We kids were dressed up like astronauts."**
b. **Roy began, "It was Halloween." "We kids were dressed up like astronauts."**

2111

pronoun 48	*She* **looked like a** *princess.* In this sentence, one italicized word is a noun, and the other is a pronoun. The pronoun is the word _____. 49
a 236	a. **The** *candy* **spoiled my appetite.** b. **The tree was decorated with** *candy* **canes.** The word *candy* is an adjective in sentence ____. 237
leaves (ones) 424	**The leaves** *on this tree* **are falling.** The prepositional phrase *on this tree* modifies the noun **leaves.** It is therefore an (*adjective, adverb*) phrase. 425
No 612	Write the correct past form of each verb in parentheses. Whenever you see the helper **have, has,** or **had,** be sure to use the helper form that ends in $-n$. I _____ (*know*) **that Carl had** _____ (*throw*) **away his ticket.** 613
a 800	In this and the following frames, underline the verb that agrees with its subject. Remember that putting an **s** on a *present* verb always makes it singular. **The fire engines** (*hurry, hurries*) **to the fire.** 801
good, well 988	**The band was** (*good, well*), **and it played** (*good, well*). 989

Yes 1176	Underline the correct pronoun: **Phil has a larger collection than** (*I, me*). 1177
who ... truck 1363	When you remove an adjective clause from a sentence, a complete sentence should remain. **The man** (*who owns the truck*) **lives across the street.** When you read this sentence without the clause, are the remaining words a sentence? (*Yes, No*) 1364
b 1550	a. **I threw the fish back into the water.** b. **And threw the fish back into the water.** The correct sentence is ____. 1551
Street Park 1737	**The Emperor Augustus ruled Rome from 27 B C to A D 14.** _____ 1738
boy's 1924	**boy's boys'** If the answer to your question is **boys,** which of the above words would you choose? _____ 1925
a 2111	a. **"Did I get any mail today?" asked Dad.** b. **"Did I get any mail today," asked Dad?** ____ 2112

She 49	Underline two pronouns that you could use to refer to yourself or your belongings. **their I mine she** 50
b 237	We have now become acquainted with four different kinds of words: *nouns, pronouns, verbs,* and _____. 238
adjective 425	a. **Several people sat** *behind us.* b. **Everyone** *behind us* **was talking.** In which sentence is the prepositional phrase an adjective phrase because it modifies a pronoun? ___ 426
knew, thrown 613	Write the correct past form of each verb in parentheses: **Jack** _____ (*grow*) **nervous because he had never** _____(*fly*) **before.** 614
hurry 801	**The chairman** (*open, opens*) **the meeting.** 802
good, well 989	**I can paint** (*good, well*) **if the brush is** (*good, well*). 990

I 1177	Underline the correct pronoun: **The storm delayed them more than it delayed** (*we, us*). 1178
Yes 1364	Add a second parenthesis [)] after the word that ends the adjective clause. Remember: If you select the clause correctly, a complete sentence should remain. **The boy (whom we chose was new to the school.** 1365
a 1551	a. **Besides being a good athlete.** b. **Jack is also a good athlete.** The correct sentence is ____. 1552
B.C. A.D. 1738	**It took Frank 7 min and 12 sec to run one mile.** _____ 1739
boys' 1925	**this girls bicycle** Whom does the **bicycle** belong to? Answer: *girl* Add the apostrophe: **this *girls* bicycle** 1926
a 2112	a. **The officer asked, "How fast were you driving"?** b. **The officer asked, "How fast were you driving?"** ____ 2113

I, mine 50	**The** *coat* **looks like** *mine*. In this sentence, the pronoun is the word _____. 51
adjectives 238	*To modify* means *to* _____ our picture or idea of something. 239
b 426	**A man** *in another car* **pointed** *to our tire*. 　　　　　a　　　　　　　　　　b Which prepositional phrase is an adverb phrase because it answers the question *Where?* about the verb? ____ 427
grew, flown 614	Write the correct past form of each verb in parentheses: **We** _____ (*throw*) **out the bread because it had** _____ (*grow*) **moldy.** 615
opens 802	**A dog or a cat** (*need, needs*) **to be trained.** 803
well, good 990	**If your work is** (*good, well*), **Mr. Brock will pay you very** (*good, well*). 991

us 1178	**The storm delayed them more than it delayed** *us*. We use the object form of the pronoun because *us* is the direct object of the verb _____. 1179
chose) 1365	Add a second parenthesis [)] after the word that ends the adjective clause: **The space (that separated the two houses was very narrow.** 1366
b 1552	a. **Which I carefully put in my pocket.** b. **I carefully put it in my pocket.** The correct sentence is ____. 1553
minutes seconds 1739	**Dr Stover shares an office with another dr in the Webster Bldg** _____ 1740
girl's 1926	**these girls bicycles** Whom do the **bicycles** belong to? Answer: *girls* Add the apostrophe: **these** *girls* **bicycles** 1927
b 2113	a. **"Safe!" called the umpire.** b. **"Safe," called the umpire!** ____ Note to student: You are now ready for Unit Test 10. 2114

mine 51	Every *car* has *one*. Which word is a pronoun because it could refer to any one of a number of things?_____ 52
change (or another word with the same meaning) 239	*gentle* **dog** In grammar, we say the adjective *gentle* _____ the noun **dog**. 240
b 427	In this and the following frames, each sentence contains one adjective phrase and one adverb phrase. **The boy** *in the next seat* **spoke** *to me*. a b The adverb phrase is (*a*, *b*). 428
threw, grown 615	Write the correct past form of each verb in parentheses: **If we had _____ (***know***) that Peter _____** (***fly***) **here, we would have picked him up at the airport.** 616
needs 803	**A dog and a cat** (*need, needs*) **to be trained.** 804
good, well 991	When the word *well* is used to mean the opposite of *sick*, it is an adjective. As an adjective, it means "in good health." **My uncle is** *well* **again.** The adjective *well* modifies the noun _____. 992

delayed 1179	Now let's abbreviate this comparison: **The storm delayed them more than it delayed** *us*. **The storm delayed them more than** *us*. We abbreviated this comparison by omitting the two words _____. 1180
houses) 1366	Add a second parenthesis [)] after the word that ends the adjective clause: **The blood (which flows from a wound washes away the germs.** 1367
b 1553	a. **Tells of an exciting adventure in a cave.** b. **The article tells of an exciting adventure in a cave.** The correct sentence is ____. 1554
Dr. doctor Building 1740	In this and the following frames, abbreviate each item as you might do to save space on a list or schedule: **Maple Road** _____ **Scott Avenue** _____ 1741
girls' 1927	**these neighbors dog** Whom does the **dog** belong to? Answer: *neighbors* Add the apostrophe: **these** *neighbors* **dog** 1928
a 2114	UNIT 11: **WHAT WORDS DO WE CAPITALIZE?** Lesson **74** **Capitals for Geographical and Group Names** *page 104* [Frames 2116-2142]

one 52	*Jack* **bought** *one* **for** *Dorothy.* In this sentence, the pronoun is the word _____. 53
modifies 240	Lesson **9** Adverbs Explain Verbs [Frames 242-277]
b 428	**The man** *across the street* **works** *for a bank.* a The adverb phrase is (*a*, *b*). 429
known, flew 616	Notice how much alike the forms of these verbs are: PRESENT SIMPLE PAST PAST WITH HELPER **tear** **tore** **(have) torn** **wear** **wore** **(have) worn** Like the other four verbs in this lesson, the helper forms of these verbs end with the letter ____. 617
need 804	**Most children** (*enjoys*, *enjoy*) **this program.** 805
uncle 992	a. **My sister cooks** *well.* b. **My sister is now** *well.* In which sentence is *well* used as an adjective? ____ 993

1180

it delayed

1181

The storm delayed them more than it delayed *us*.
The storm delayed them more than *us*.

When we omit the words **it delayed,** do we still use the same form of the pronoun? (*Yes, No*)

1367

wound)

1368

ADJECTIVE CLAUSE SIGNALS: **who (whom, whose),**
which, that

There are many plants which will bloom indoors.

The adjective clause starts with the word _____

and ends with the word _____.

1554

b

Lesson **54** A Closer Look at Sentence Fragments

[Frames 1556-1588]

1741

Maple Rd.
Scott Ave.

1742

Sunday _____

Monday _____

1928

neighbors'

1929

our doctors car

Whom does the **car** belong to? Answer: *doctor*

Add the apostrophe:

our *doctors* car

Capital letters are a helpful guide to the reader.

Have you ever seen John cook?
Have you ever seen John Cook?

The meaning of these sentences depends on whether or not you capitalize the letter ____.

2116

one	A word used in place of a noun is a _____.
53	54

What kind?   Which one(s)?   How many?   How much?
In the last lesson we learned that words that answer these
questions about nouns are called _____.

242

---

b	*Through the telescope* **I could see the outline** *of a ship.* 　　　　a　　　　　　　　　　　　　　　　　　　　　b The adverb phrase is (*a*, *b*).
429	430

−n	PRESENT　　　SIMPLE PAST　　　PAST WITH HELPER 　**tear**　　　　　**tore**　　　　　　**(have) torn** Write the correct past forms of **tear**: **My sleeve _____ in the same place that it had _____ before.**
617	618

---

enjoy	**The old house** (*looks*, *look*) **deserted.**
805	806

---

b	**Grandma Smith had an operation, but she is now** *well.* In this sentence, *well* is used as an (*adjective*, *adverb*).
993	994

Yes 1181	In any abbreviated comparison, think of the omitted word or words. This will tell you immediately which form of the pronoun to use. **I am two inches taller than .?. (is).** Think of the omitted word *is*. Which pronoun would fit in this sentence—**he** or **him?**_____ 1182
which ... indoors 1368	**The man who gave us our directions forgot to mention the turn.** The adjective clause starts with the word _____ and ends with the word _____. 1369
	To make sense, you must name what you are talking about. This is the subject part of your sentence. After you name what you are talking about, you must say something about it. This is the verb part of your sentence. **My <u>dad</u> <u>closed</u> the door and <u>locked</u> it.** How many verbs say something about the subject? _____ 1556
Sun. **Mon.** 1742	**January** _____ **February** _____ 1743
doctor's 1929	Remember that the word *before* the apostrophe should always name the owner or owners. a. **the** *lady's* **rings** b. **the** *ladies'* **rings** Look at the word before the apostrophe. Which example means the **rings** of *one* lady? _____ 1930
c 2116	**boy Harold** One of these nouns can be applied to *any* boy; the other noun names *one particular* boy that we might be talking about. The noun that names *one particular* boy is _____. 2117

pronoun	A pronoun is (*more, less*) definite than a noun.
54	55

adjectives	We need a different kind of word to explain more about the actions of verbs.
	
	    a. **The bus turned.**
	    b. **The bus turned** *sharply.*
	
	Which sentence gives you a clearer idea of the action of the verb **turned?** ____

242	243

a	**Ships** <u>*from many countries*</u> **dock** <u>*in San Francisco Bay.*</u> a b The adverb phrase is (*a, b*).
430	431

tore, torn	PRESENT SIMPLE PAST PAST WITH HELPER **wear** **wore** **(have) worn** Write the correct past forms of **wear:** **Sandra** _____ **the same dress that she had** _____ **to my party.**
618	619

looks	**Rain and sunshine** (*make, makes*) **plants grow.**
806	807

adjective	**I slept . . . .** **Sue dances . . . .** **Ray bats . . . .** **The corn grows . . . .** To complete all these sentences, you would use the adverb (*good, well*).
994	995

<table>
<tr><td>

he

1182
</td><td>

I am two inches taller than *he* **(is).**

We use the subject form *he* because it is the subject of the omitted verb _____.

1183
</td></tr>
<tr><td>

who ... directions

1369
</td><td>

Few city dogs get the exercise that they need.

The adjective clause starts with the word _____ and ends with the word _____.

1370
</td></tr>
<tr><td>

two

1556
</td><td>

My dad closed the door and locked it.

Both the verb **closed** and the verb **locked** say something about the subject _____.

1557
</td></tr>
<tr><td>

Jan.
Feb.

1743
</td><td>

Father Brady _____

Professor Morris _____

1744
</td></tr>
<tr><td>

a

1930
</td><td>

the *lady's* **rings**

This means the **rings** of *one* lady because the word before the apostrophe is _____.

1931
</td></tr>
<tr><td>

Harold

2117
</td><td>

a. **Canada**   b. **country**

The noun that names *one particular* country is _____.

2118
</td></tr>
</table>

less 55	We have now studied two different kinds of words, _____ and _____. 56
b 243	**turned** *sharply* **turned** *suddenly* **turned** *slowly* Each pair of words gives you a different idea of *how* the bus **turned.** The word that changes your idea is the (*first, second*) word in each pair. 244
b 431	<u>*During the week*</u> **I read a book** <u>*about deep-sea diving.*</u> a b The adverb phrase is (*a, b*). 432
wore, worn 619	Here are the simple past forms of the 13 verbs that you studied in this and the previous lesson: **drove spoke took fell broke wrote ate** **flew grew knew threw tore wore** Do any of these verbs have a past form that ends in *–ed*? (*Yes, No*) 620
make 807	**A book or a magazine** (*help, helps*) **to pass the time.** 808
well 995	Lesson **34** The Problem of *Sense* Verbs [Frames 997-1028]

is 1183	**The doctor charged us more than** (*he charged*) .?.. Think of the omitted words *he charged.* Which pronoun would fit in this sentence—**they** or **them**? _____ 1184
that ... need 1370	**We called a doctor whom a neighbor had recommended.** The adjective clause starts with the word _____ and ends with the word _____. 1371
dad 1557	WRONG: **My dad closed the door.** *And locked it.* The italicized word group is a fragment, not a sentence. It is a fragment because it lacks a (*subject, verb*). 1558
Fr. Brady Prof. Morris 1744	**Fisher Building** _____ **Ford Motor Company** _____ 1745
lady (*or* singular) 1931	the *ladies'* rings This means the **rings** of *more than one* lady because the word before the apostrophe is _____. 1932
Canada 2118	a. **city** b. **Los Angeles** The noun that names *one particular* city is _____. 2119

Lesson 3 Verbs Supply the Action

[Frames 58-85]

---

second

244

The *green* **bus turned** *sharply.*

The adjective *green* modifies the noun **bus.**

Which word modifies the verb **turned?** _____.

245

---

a

432

You often find two phrases in a row. The second phrase may modify the object of the first phrase, or it may modify the verb in another part of the sentence.

We learn much history *from the letters* *of soldiers.*
                                  a   b

Phrase *b* modifies (*learn, letters*).

433

No

620

Here are the helper forms of the same verbs:

(have) driv<u>en</u>   (have) spok<u>en</u>   (have) tak<u>en</u>   (have) fall<u>en</u>
(have) brok<u>en</u>   (have) writt<u>en</u>   (have) eat<u>en</u>   (have) flow<u>n</u>
(have) grow<u>n</u>   (have) know<u>n</u>   (have) throw<u>n</u>   (have) tor<u>n</u>
(have) wor<u>n</u>

Each of these helper forms ends with the two letters ____ or the letter ____.

621

---

helps

808

Lesson 27 *Doesn't and Don't; Was and Were*

[Frames 810-841]

---

      look   **feel**   **taste**   **smell**   **hear**
All these verbs are connected with our senses.

Each one of these verbs can mean an action we perform with parts of our bodies. For example, we **look** with our eyes, **feel** with our hands, and **smell** with our _____.

997

them 1184	So far, we have looked at comparisons made with the word **than.** Comparisons made with the word **as** are no different. **They can't stay as long as .?. (can stay).** Think of the omitted words *can stay.* Which pronoun would fit in this sentence—**we** or **us?** _____ 1185
whom ... recommended 1371	**The page which was missing from my book was found on the floor.** The adjective clause starts with the word _____ and ends with the word _____. 1372
subject 1558	When a sentence has two verbs that say different things about the same subject, don't cut off one of the verbs. a. **I like our new house but miss my old friends.** b. **I like our new house. But miss my old friends.** In which line do you find a sentence fragment? ____ 1559
Fisher Bldg. Ford Motor Co. 1745	Lesson **61** **Commas in Compound Sentences** [Frames 1747-1777]
ladies (*or* plural) 1932	a. **All the *baby's* diets are carefully checked.** b. **All the *babies'* diets are carefully checked.** c. **All the *babie's* diets are carefully checked.** Which sentence is correct? ____ 1933
Los Angeles 2119	boy　　　country　　city Harold　　Canada　　Los Angeles We capitalize nouns that apply to (*any, a particular*) one of their kind. 2120

To make a sentence, you must first have a subject to talk about.

Herb   school   football   happiness

Does each of these words name a subject that you could make a sentence about? *(Yes, No)*

58

---

sharply

245

A word that modifies a verb is called an **adverb.**

The green bus turned *sharply.*

Because it modifies the verb **turned,** the word *sharply* is an _____.

246

---

letters

433

Remember: If a phrase can be moved to another part of the sentence, it modifies the verb.

I put the box <u>*of matches*</u> <u>*on a high shelf.*</u>
                          a   b

Phrase b modifies (*put, matches*).

434

–en, –n

621

A common mistake is to use the simple past form of these verbs, instead of the helper forms, after **have, has,** or **had.**

      a. **Dave** *has tore* **his shirt.**
      b. **Dave** *has torn* **his shirt.**

Which sentence is correct? ____

622

SINGULAR: **This <u>watch runs.</u>**

PLURAL: **These <u>watches run.</u>**

When we add an **s** to a verb that shows *present* time, we always make the verb (*singular, plural*).

810

---

noses

997

look   feel   taste   smell   hear

When these verbs are used to mean actions, we would use (*adjectives, adverbs*) to describe *how* these actions are performed.

998

My perfect score on the test surprised my teacher as well as (*it surprised*) .?. .

Think of the omitted words *it surprised*.
Which pronoun would fit in this sentence—**I** or **me**? _____

We finally found the man whose car had rolled into the street.

The adjective clause starts with the word _____

and ends with the word _____.

---

a. **Roy must pay a fine or lose his driver's license.**
b. **Roy must pay a fine. Or lose his driver's license.**

Which arrangement is correct? _____ .

A compound sentence is made by joining two separate sentences. We use the conjunction **and, but,** or **or** to combine them.

   We talked to the pilot, *and* we asked many questions.

The conjunction that connects the two parts of this compound sentence is _____.

The words **man** and **woman** are singular; the words **men** and **women** are plural.

a. **the man's score**
b. **the men's score**

Which means the score of *more than one* man? _____

All the rules for capitals are based on one simple idea: Use a capital letter (or letters) for the special name of *one particular* person, group of people, place, or thing.

a. **people**   b. **Eskimos**

The noun that is the name of *one particular* group of people is _____.

Yes

Herb   school   football   happiness

Does any one of these words by itself make a complete sentence? *(Yes, No)*

58

59

---

adverb

Pete studied.

This sentence tells you that Pete **studied**—nothing more. Here are questions you might ask about Pete's action:

When?   Where?   How?   How often?

Any word that would answer one of these questions would be an *(adjective, adverb)*.

246

247

---

put

He wrote the poem *on the back of an envelope.*
                                     a   b

Phrase *b* modifies *(wrote, back)*.

434

435

---

b

It is simple to avoid this mistake. Whenever you need a helper form of one of these verbs, ask yourself if the verb has a form that ends in *–n* or *–en*.

Does the verb **throw** have an *–n* or an *–en* form? *(Yes, No)*

622

623

---

singular

This girl does the typing.

This sentence is correct because the singular verb **does** agrees with the singular subject **girl**.

We know that **does** is singular because it ends in ____.

810

811

---

adverbs

The customer *looked* **carefully at his change.**

In this sentence, *looked* means an action of the eyes.

To describe this action, we use the adverb _____.

998

999

me
 	
1186
	Sometimes the meaning of a sentence depends on whether we use the subject or object form of a pronoun.
	
	  a. **Dad helps my sister more than <u>I</u>** (*help her*).
	  b. **Dad helps my sister more than** (*he helps*) **<u>me</u>**.
	
	In which sentence is the underlined pronoun the subject of the omitted verb? _____
	
	1187

whose ... street 1373	**A person who weighs 150 pounds on the earth would weigh only 25 pounds on the moon.** The adjective clause starts with the word _____ and ends with the word _____. 1374
a 1560	a. **My dog comes** *promptly*. b. **My dog comes** *when I call him*. Sentence *a* contains an adverb. Sentence *b* contains an adverb clause. Both the adverb and the adverb clause tell *when* about the verb _____, which they modify. 1561
and 1747	**I recognized Pauline,** *but* **she didn't recognize me.** The conjunction that connects the two parts of this compound sentence is _____. 1748
b 1934	a. **the women's pay** b. **the woman's pay** Which means the pay of *more than one* woman? _____ 1935
Eskimos 2121	Here is our first rule for using capitals: Capitalize geographical names that apply to *particular* countries, states, cities, streets, and so forth. **state Ohio** The noun that names *one particular* place is _____. 2122

No	**Herb laughed.** Now this is a sentence because we have added the word _____.
59	60

adverb	**Pete studied** *hard.* The adverb *hard* modifies the verb **studied.** Underline the question it answers: **How? Where? When?**
247	248

back	**I carried the letter** <u>*in my pocket*</u> <u>*for several days.*</u> a b Phrase *b* modifies (*carried, pocket*).
435	436

Yes	a. **The pitcher** *had thrown* **a wild pitch.** b. **The pitcher** *had threw* **a wild pitch.** Which sentence is correct? _____
623	624

s	a. **This <u>girl</u> <u>does</u> not <u>type</u>.** b. **This <u>girl</u> <u>do</u> not <u>type</u>.** Which sentence is correct because the subject and the verb agree in number? _____
811	812

carefully	**I** *felt* **the hot stove cautiously.** In this sentence, *felt* means an action of the hands. To describe this action, we use the adverb _____.
999	1000

a 1187	a. **Dad helps my sister more than I** (*help her*). b. **Dad helps my sister more than** (*he helps*) **me**. In which sentence is the underlined pronoun the direct object of the omitted verb? ____ 1188
who ... earth 1374	**A family that lives on a houseboat can move very easily.** The adjective clause starts with the word _____ and ends with the word _____. 1375
comes 1561	**My dog comes.** *Promptly.* Is it correct to cut off the adverb *promptly* from the verb **comes,** which it modifies? (*Yes, No*) 1562
but 1748	**I call for Bob,** *or* **Bob calls for me.** The conjunction that connects the two parts of this compound sentence is _____. 1749
a 1935	The word **child** is singular; the word **children** is plural. a. **Here are the** *childrens'* **magazines.** b. **Here are the** *children's* **magazines.** The *magazines* belong to the *children*. Which sentence is correct? ____ 1936
Ohio 2122	a. **country** **state** **city** **street** b. **france** **oregon** **denver** **broadway** In which group should the words be written with capital letters? ____ 2123

laughed 60	**Herb laughed.** The word **laughed** tells what **Herb** did. Any word that tells what someone or something *does* is called a **verb.** The word **laughed** in this sentence is a _____. 61
How? 248	**Pete studied** *yesterday.* The adverb *yesterday* modifies the verb **studied.** Underline the question it answers: **How?** **Where?** **When?** 249
carried 436	**You can see cottages** *across the lake* *on clear days.* 　　　　　　　　　　　　　　a　　　　　　　b Phrase *b* modifies (*can see, lake*). 437
a 624	You know that after any form of **have (has, had)** you must use the helper form of the verb. After any form of **be (is, am, are—was, were, been),** you must use the helper form, too. Use the helper form of the verb after any form of the helping verb *have* or _____. 625
a 812	We can make one word of **does not** by writing **doesn't.** We can make one word of **do not** by writing **don't.** The verb **don't** can be either singular or plural—for example, "I don't" (singular), "We don't" (plural). The verb **doesn't,** however, is always _____. 813.
cautiously 1000	**Marjorie** *tasted* **her first cake hopefully.** In this sentence, *tasted* means an action of the mouth. To describe this action, we use the adverb _____. 1001

a. **Dad helps my sister more than** I (*help her*).
b. **Dad helps my sister more than** (*he helps*) *me*.

Which sentence means that your dad gives more help to your sister than you do? ____

We were asked to write a theme about any person whom we admired.

The adjective clause starts with the word _____

and ends with the word _____.

My dog comes. *When I call him.*

Is it correct to cut off the adverb clause *when I call him* from the verb **comes,** which it modifies? (*Yes, No*)

The three conjunctions that can join two sentences into a compound sentence are _____, _____, and _____.

---

a. **Some** *children's* **games are very interesting.**
b. **Some** *childrens'* **games are very interesting.**

Which sentence is correct? ____

Copy and add capital letters to the two words which should be capitalized:

We left detroit and crossed the river to canada.

_____

verb 61	**Herb laughed.** Underline two other verbs that could tell what **Herb** did: **shouted** **tall** **stumbled** **soon** 62
When? 249	**Pete studied** *there.* The adverb *there* modifies the verb **studied.** Underline the question it answers: **How often?** **Where?** **How?** 250
can see 437	Lesson **15** **Conjunctions Do the Connecting** [Frames 439-470]
be 625	a. **This wedding dress** *was wore* **by my grandmother.** b. **This wedding dress** *was worn* **by my grandmother.** Which sentence is correct? ____ 626
singular 813	Use **doesn't** only where you can use the words **does not.** Use **don't** only where you can use the words ____ ____. 814
hopefully 1001	**look** **feel** **taste** **smell** These verbs have a second meaning. This meaning has nothing to do with actions of our eyes, hands, noses, and mouths. **The pie** *looks* **good.** Does a pie have eyes with which to look at something? (*Yes, No*) 1002

a

1189

a. **Dad helps my sister more than** *I* (*help her*).
b. **Dad helps my sister more than** (*he helps*) *me*.

Which sentence means that your dad helps both your

sister and you but that he helps her more? _____

1190

---

whom . . . admired

1376

No

1563

A word group and the word it modifies should always be
(*in the same sentence, in different sentences*).

1564

---

and, but, or

1750

We talked to the pilot, *and* **we asked many questions.**

In a compound sentence, are there a subject and a verb
both *before* and *after* the conjunction? (*Yes, No*)

1751

---

a

1937

In this and the following frames, add the apostrophe in
each italicized word. Be sure to ask your question in exactly these words: "Whom (*or* What) does it belong to?"
Using other words can give you the wrong answer.

One *boys* **locker wouldn't open.**

1938

Detroit, Canada

2124

Also capitalize the complete names of *particular* oceans,
lakes, rivers, mountains, parks, and so forth.
When a word such as **ocean, lake, river,** or **park** is part of
the complete name, this word should be capitalized, too.

a. **Columbia River**   b. **Columbia river**

Which example is correctly capitalized? _____

2125

shouted,
stumbled

62

Herb laughed.

Whom or what is this two-word sentence about? _____

63

Where?

250

---

a. **Our boat leaks** *now.*
b. **Our boat leaks** *badly.*
c. **Our boat leaks** *everywhere.*

All the italicized words are adverbs because they modify

the verb _____.

251

Wendy and Stan washed the dishes.

This sentence has two (*subjects, verbs*).

439

---

b

626

The following frames review the irregular verbs in this and
the previous lesson. In each frame, write the correct past
forms of the verbs in parentheses:

My Uncle Mac _____ (*drive*) to Milwaukee and

_____ (*fly*) **back.**

627

---

do not

814

My dad *don't* **smoke.**

In this sentence, could you use the words *do not* instead
of *don't*? (*Yes, No*)

815

No

1002

These melons *feel* **ripe.**

Does a melon have hands with which to feel something?
(*Yes, No*)

1003

Ann writes to Verna as often as (*she, her*).

To say that Ann writes to Verna as often as another girl writes to Verna, choose the pronoun (*she, her*).

b

1190

1191

I have a cousin *who visits my sister.*

The adjective clause *who visits my sister* modifies the noun _____.

1378

---

in the same sentence

If a clause is cut off from the word it modifies, it becomes a sentence fragment. Let's see why:

WRONG: **My dog comes.** *When I call him.*

Although the clause *When I call him* has a subject and a verb, does it make sense by itself? (*Yes, No*)

1564

1565

Yes

If you don't find a subject and a verb after the conjunction, is it a compound sentence? (*Yes, No*)

1751

1752

---

boy's

(Whom do the **parents** belong to?)

Several *students* **parents visited our class.**

1938

1939

---

a

a. **Yellowstone national park**   b. **Yellowstone National Park**

Which example is correctly capitalized? ____

2125

2126

Herb 63	The word that names *whom* or *what* a sentence is about is called the **subject** of the sentence. **Herb laughed.** **Fred laughed.** **Judy laughed.** Each of these sentences has a different _____. 64

leaks
 	
251
	Adverbs, like adjectives, can answer the question *How much?*
	
	    a. **Our boat leaks** *now.*
	    b. **Our boat leaks** *badly.*
	    c. **Our boat leaks** *everywhere.*
	In which sentence does the italicized adverb answer the question *How much?* ____
	
	252

subjects 439	**Wendy and Stan washed the dishes.** The two subjects, **Wendy** and **Stan**, are connected by the word _____. 440
drove, flew 627	Keep your eyes open for forms of the helping verbs **have (has, had)** and **be (is, am, are—was, were, been).** Be sure to use the helper form (*–n* or *–en*) after them. **The children** _____ (*grow*) **sleepy soon after they had** _____ (*eat*) **their dinner.** 628
No 815	a. **My dad** *don't* **smoke.** b. **My dad** *doesn't* **smoke.** Which sentence is correct? ____ 816
No 1003	**My apple** *tastes* **sour.** Does an apple have a mouth with which to taste something? (*Yes, No*) 1004

she 1191	**Ann writes to Verna as often as** (*she, her*). To say that Ann writes to Verna as often as Ann writes to another girl, choose the pronoun (*she, her*). 1192
cousin 1378	**I have a cousin** *who visits my sister*. The clause signal *who* is a pronoun. It refers to the noun _____. 1379
No 1565	WRONG: *When I call him.* This clause by itself doesn't satisfy you. You want to hear *what happens*. When you write a clause as though it were a complete sentence, you produce a sentence _____. 1566
No 1752	**We talked to the pilot** *and* **we asked many questions.** Listen to yourself say this sentence. Notice where your voice pauses. Your voice pauses after the noun _____. 1753
students' 1939	(Whom did the **handkerchief** belong to?) **A** *mans* **handkerchief is the only clue.** 1940
b 2126	Copy and add capital letters to the three words which should be capitalized: **The Erie canal connects the Hudson river with lake Erie.** _____ 2127

subject 64	**Herb laughed.** **Herb shouted.** **Herb stumbled.** Each of these sentences has a different _____. 65
b 252	a. **Our boat leaks** *now.* b. **Our boat leaks** *badly.* c. **Our boat leaks** *everywhere.* In which sentence does the italicized adverb answer the question *When?* ___ 253
and 440	**Wendy washed and dried the dishes.** This sentence has two (*subjects, verbs*). 441
grew, eaten 628	**These strawberries are** _____ (*grow*) **in California** **and are** _____ (*fly*) **to the East.** 629
b 816	a. **The bus** *doesn't* **stop here.** b. **The bus** *don't* **stop here.** Which sentence is correct? ___ 817
No 1004	Do you remember that there are two kinds of verbs— *action* verbs and *linking* verbs? The job of a *linking* verb is to connect a word that follows it with the subject. **The pie is good.** What is the linking verb that connects the adjective **good** with the subject **pie?** ___ 1005

her 1192	In this and the following frames, underline the correct pronoun in each comparison. Be sure to think of the missing words before making your choice. **We made two more touchdowns than** (*they, them*). 1193
cousin 1379	Here is the adjective clause by itself: *who visits my sister* The subject of the verb *visits* is the pronoun _____. 1380
fragment 1566	a. **I am interested in stamps. Although I don't collect them.** b. **I am interested in stamps although I don't collect them.** Which arrangement is correct? ____ 1567
pilot 1753	In a compound sentence, put a comma after the first part of the sentence, where your voice pauses. This comma separates the two parts of the sentence and makes the sentence easier to read. **We talked to the pilot,** *and* **we asked many questions.** The comma comes (*before, after*) the conjunction **and.** 1754
man's 1940	(Whom do the **children** belong to?) **My two** *sisters* **children are all boys.** 1941
Canal, River, Lake 2127	Capitalize the word **street, avenue, road, drive, boulevard,** and so forth, when it is part of the complete name. **Main Street Sanford Avenue Wilshire Boulevard** Supply capitals for the four words that need them. **Our school is at the corner of curtis street and pine road.** 2128

verb	**He laughed.** **She shouted.** **We stumbled.** Can pronouns, as well as nouns, be the subjects of sentences? *(Yes, No)*
65	66

a	a. **Our boat leaks** *now.* b. **Our boat leaks** *badly.* c. **Our boat leaks** *everywhere.* In which sentence does the italicized adverb answer the question *Where?* _____
253	254

verbs	**Wendy** <u>**washed**</u> **and** <u>**dried**</u> **the dishes.** The two verbs, **washed** and **dried**, are connected by the word _____.
441	442

grown, flown	**Ross must have** _____ *(know)* **that his shirt was** _____ *(tear).*
629	630

a	a. **He . . . like cats.** b. **They . . . like cats.** In which sentence would **don't** be correct because the words **do not** would fit in? _____
817	818

is	**These melons are ripe.** What is the linking verb that connects the adjective **ripe** with the subject **melons?** _____
1005	1006

they 1193	**This coat fits you better than** (*she, her*). 1194
who 1380	**Who** (like **he**) is the subject form of the pronoun. **Whom** (like **him**) is the object form of the pronoun. When the pronoun is the subject of the verb, you would choose (*who, whom*). 1381
b 1567	a. **Ellen wrote a poem, which the teacher read to the class.** b. **Ellen wrote a poem. Which the teacher read to the class.** Which arrangement is correct? ____ 1568
before 1754	The comma in a compound sentence helps you to read it more easily and to get the right meaning. **Jim apologized to Sue and his mother was pleased.** Because the comma is missing from this sentence, you might get the idea that Jim apologized to two persons— **Sue** and _____. 1755
sisters' 1941	(Whom do the **records** belong to?) **Each** *pupils* **records are kept in the office.** 1942
Curtis Street, Pine Road 2128	Copy and add capital letters to the four words which should be capitalized: **Our street will be paved from madison avenue to sunset drive.** 2129

Yes 66	a. **Herb laughed.** b. **They shouted.** c. **Judy stumbled.** In which sentence is the subject a pronoun? ____ 67

c
 	
254
	Now, for just a few frames, let's go back to adjectives.
	
	    a. **Roy lives in the** *white* **house.**
	    b. **The band played** *several* **pieces.**
	    c. **Floyd showed** *great* **courage.**
	
	Is each italicized adjective right next to the word it modifies? (*Yes, No*)
	
	255

and 442	**Wendy or Stan washed the dishes.** Here the two subjects, **Wendy** and **Stan**, are connected by the word _____. 443
known, torn 630	**The clerk** _____ (*throw*) **away the cookies that had** _____ (*fall*) **on the floor.** 631
b 818	**.?.** *don't* **look fresh.** Underline two items that could be used correctly as the subject of the above sentence. Remember that *don't* means *do not.* **The lettuce The carrots It They** 819
are 1006	The most common linking verb is **be** (*is, am, are—was, were, been*). **These melons are ripe.** Two of the following verbs could be used in place of the linking verb **are** in the above sentence. Underline these two verbs: **look walk feel fix** 1007

her 1194	Dad doesn't have as much patience as (*she, her*). 1195
who 1381	When the pronoun is the object of the verb, you would choose (*who, whom*). 1382
a 1568	Don't cut off an *–ing* word group from the sentence that contains the word it modifies. WRONG: **Tommy burst into the house. Waving his report card proudly.** The sentence fragment is the (*first, second*) word group. 1569
(his) mother 1755	Punctuate this compound sentence: **The air was cold but the water was warm.** 1756
pupil's 1942	**The two *mens* fingerprints were compared.** 1943
Madison Avenue, Sunset Drive 2129	Here is another rule for using capital letters: Capitalize nouns and adjectives that apply to *particular* nationalities, languages, races, and religious groups. **Canadian French Negro Catholic** Which word is the name of both a nationality and a language? _____ 2130

b 67	**Herb laughed.** **Herb shouted.** **Herb stumbled.** In all these sentences, do the verbs show action that you might plainly see? *(Yes, No)* 68
Yes 255	a. **Roy lives in the** *white* **house.** b. **The band played** *several* **pieces.** c. **Floyd showed** *great* **courage.** Can the italicized adjectives be moved to other positions in these sentences? *(Yes, No)* 256
or 443	**We listened but heard nothing.** This sentence has two *(subjects, verbs)*. 444
threw, fallen 631	**The car could be _____ (*drive*) even though the** **windshield was _____ (*break*).** 632
The carrots, **They** 819	**.?. *don't* fit well.** Underline two items that could be used correctly as the subject of the above sentence: **The coat The sleeves My shoes The collar** 820
look, feel 1007	**These melons are ripe.** Underline two more verbs that could be used in place of the linking verb **are:** **plant taste find smell** 1008

she 1195	Although Cliff has collected stamps for only a short time, he already has more stamps than (*I, me*). (Are you thinking of the missing words?) 1196
whom 1382	**I have a cousin** *who visits* **my sister.** In the adjective clause, we use the subject form *who* because it is the subject of the verb _____. 1383
second 1569	Here is the *–ing* word group by itself: 　　FRAGMENT: *Waving his report card proudly.* Does this *–ing* word group have both a subject and a verb? (*Yes, No*) 1570
cold, but 1756	Punctuate this compound sentence: 　　**You must hire a guide or you might lose your way.** 1757
men's 1943	**This author writes** *childrens* **books.** 1944
French 2130	**Cuban　　Negro　　Baptist** Which word is the name of a particular race? _____ 2131

Yes
 	
68
	There are other actions that are not so easy to see because they occur within a person's mind.
	
	     a. **Herb jumped.**
	     b. **Herb thought.**
	
	In which sentence does the verb express an action of the mind? ____
	
	69

No 256	An adjective usually cannot be moved from its position before the noun it modifies. Now look at an adverb: **Don visits me** *frequently.* The word *frequently* is an adverb because it modifies the verb _____. 257
verbs 444	**We listened but heard nothing.** The two verbs, **listened** and **heard**, are connected by the word _____. 445
driven, broken 632	**Some of us _____ (***know***) that the poem had been _____ (***write***) by Phyllis.** 633
The sleeves, My shoes 820	When you use **doesn't** or **don't** to ask a question, look ahead to see whether the subject is singular or plural. If the subject is singular, use (*doesn't, don't*). 821
taste, smell 1008	**These melons (look, feel, taste, or smell) ripe.** Whichever one of these verbs you used would connect the adjective **ripe** with the subject _____. 1009

I	**Bobby is jealous because he thinks his parents like the baby more than** (*he, him*).
1196	1197

visits	Now we shall change the meaning of our clause: **I have a cousin** *whom my <u>sister</u> <u>visits</u>.* In the adjective clause, the subject of the verb *visits* is not *whom,* but _____.
1383	1384

No	FRAGMENT: *Waving his report card proudly.* Does this *–ing* word group make sense by itself? (*Yes, No*)
1570	1571

guide, or	A sentence is not compound unless there are a subject and a verb both *before* and *after* the conjunction. Look carefully at this sentence: **We <u>talked</u> to the pilot** *and* **<u>asked</u> many questions.** After the conjunction *and,* do you find both a subject and a verb? (*Yes, No*)
1757	1758

children's	In each of the remaining frames, there are two italicized words that require apostrophes. **My** *fathers* **job was to collect all the** *members* **dues.**
1944	1945

Negro	**Polish Indian Jewish** Which adjective applies to a particular religious group? _____
2131	2132

b 69	Underline two verbs that express actions of the mind: **played agreed wondered pitched** 70
visits 257	a. **Don visits me** *frequently.* b. **Don** *frequently* **visits me.** c. *Frequently* **Don visits me.** Is an adverb always next to the verb it modifies? *(Yes, No)* 258
but 445	Words used to connect words or groups of words are called **conjunctions.** The most common conjunctions are **and, but,** and **or.** We use conjunctions to _____ words or groups of words. 446
knew, written 633	**Miss Daly had _____ (***speak***) to me about the test** **I had _____ (***take***) on Monday.** 634
doesn't 821	a. ... that cake look good? b. ... those cookies look good? In which sentence would it be a mistake to use the plural verb **Don't?** ___ 822
melons 1009	Every linking verb is followed by a word that refers back to the subject. Early in this book, we learned that this word is called a **subject complement.** **These melons are ripe.** The subject complement **ripe** describes the _____. 1010

him 1197	Canada has as high a standard of living as (*we, us*). 1198
sister 1384	*whom my sister visits* Now let's straighten out this clause, remembering that *whom* stands for *cousin*. *my sister visits whom* The clause signal *whom* is the direct _____ of the verb *visits*. 1385
No 1571	a. **Knowing nothing about the party. I walked into the room.** b. **Knowing nothing about the party, I walked into the room.** Which arrangement is correct? ____ 1572
No 1758	**We talked to the pilot** *and* **asked many questions.** After the conjunction *and*, we do not find both a subject and a verb. We find only a (*subject, verb*). 1759
father's, members' 1945	**Two other** *boys* **scores were higher than** *Carls* **score.** 1946
Jewish 2132	Copy and add capital letters to the three words which should be capitalized: The spanish conquerors converted many indians to the catholic faith. 2133

agreed, wondered	Underline two verbs that express actions of the mind: **hoped pushed feared returned**
70	71

No	You will often find an adverb several words away from the verb it modifies. *Recently* **one of my friends** *moved.* How many words come between the adverb and the verb it modifies? _____
258	259

connect (*or* join)	You will have no trouble spelling the first and last syllable of the word *con-junc-tion.* Fill in the middle syllable: *con_____tion.*
446	447

spoken, taken	Lesson **21** Verbs of the *Ring–Rang–Rung* Pattern [Frames 636-661]
634	

a	Underline the correct verb: (*Doesn't, Don't*) **that window open?**
822	823

melons	**These melons look ripe. These melons taste ripe.** **These melons feel ripe. These melons smell ripe.** In each of these sentences, too, the subject complement **ripe** describes the subject _____.
1010	1011

we 1198	We are not at home as much as (*they, them*). 1199
object 1385	It is very easy to decide whether to use *who* or *whom* as an adjective clause signal. <u>who</u> <u>visits</u> *my sister* If the verb has no other possible subject, use _____. 1386
b 1572	When appositives are cut off from the words they explain, they, too, become fragments. WRONG: **We spoke to Mr. Fry.** *The owner of the lot.* The appositive word group *The owner of the lot* belongs in the same sentence with the name _____, which it explains. 1573
verb 1759	<u>We</u> <u>talked</u> to the pilot *and* <u>asked</u> many questions. Is this sentence compound? (*Yes, No*) 1760
boys', Carl's 1946	My youngest *sisters* hobby is collecting movie *actors* pictures. 1947
Spanish, Indians, Catholic 2133	Copy and add capital letters to the three words which should be capitalized: **Many american and european composers have been influenced by negro music.** 2134

hoped, feared 71	A verb that expresses action of any kind—whether you can see it or not—is called an **action verb**. **slipped dreamed escaped understood** Are all these verbs *action verbs*? (Yes, No) 72
four 259	In this and the following frames, you will find one or more words separating the adverb from the verb it modifies. Circle the verb and underline the adverb that modifies it: **Suddenly the chair collapsed.** 260
junc 447	Underline two conjunctions in this sentence: **Any boy or girl will understand and enjoy this story.** 448
	All five verbs in this lesson follow the same pattern: PRESENT: **r<u>i</u>ng s<u>i</u>ng sw<u>i</u>m dr<u>i</u>nk beg<u>i</u>n** SIMPLE PAST: **r<u>a</u>ng s<u>a</u>ng sw<u>a</u>m dr<u>a</u>nk beg<u>a</u>n** When we change these verbs from present to simple past, the *i* in each verb changes to ____. 636
Doesn't 823	*WAS* AND *WERE* Here are two sentences that show *present* time: SINGULAR: **The car stops.** PLURAL: **The cars stop.** When we change the subject from singular to plural, do we need to change the verb? (Yes, No) 824
melons 1011	**These melons look ripe. These melons taste ripe.** **These melons feel ripe. These melons smell ripe.** The subject **melons** is a noun. Therefore, the subject complement **ripe**, which describes it, must be an (*adverb, adjective*). 1012

they 1199	Although Gerald worked a shorter time, Mr. Davis paid him just as much as (*I, me*). 1200
who 1386	*whom my sister visits* If the verb has another word as its subject, use _____. 1387
Mr. Fry 1573	Here is the appositive phrase by itself: FRAGMENT: *The owner of the lot.* Does this word group have both a subject and a verb, or does it express a complete thought? (*Yes, No*) 1574
No 1760	**We talked to the pilot *and* asked many questions.** This sentence is not compound. The *and* does not connect two sentences, each with its own subject and verb. The conjunction *and* connects the two verbs **talked** and _____. 1761
sister's, actors' 1947	All the *childrens* **parents met in the** *schools* **auditorium.** 1948
American, European, Negro 2134	In this and the following frames, copy only the words in which the small letters should be changed to capitals. Add the necessary capitals. (The number after each sentence tells how many words need to be capitalized.) **The restaurant on dorset avenue serves excellent chinese food. (3)** _____ 2135

Yes

To identify the subject and verb of a sentence, we shall underline the subject with one line and the verb with two lines.

Underline the subject and verb in this sentence:

Parrots talk.

72

73

---

suddenly

(collapsed)

Circle the verb and underline the adverb that modifies it:

I shook the rug vigorously.

260

261

---

or, and

Underline two conjunctions in this sentence:

The sandwiches and desserts are cheap but good.

448

449

---

a

Underline three verbs that show past time:

ring   sang   swam   drink   began

636

637

Yes

Now we shall change these same sentences to show *past* time:

SINGULAR: **The car stopped.**
PLURAL: **The cars stopped.**

When we change the subject from singular to plural, do we still need to change the verb? (*Yes, No*)

824

825

---

adjective

These melons are ripe.

We have seen that the verbs **look, feel, taste,** and **smell** could be used as linking verbs in the above sentence.

In different sentences, could these same verbs be used to show actions of our eyes, hands, noses, and mouths? (*Yes, No*)

1012

1013

Lesson 41 Four Pronoun Problems

[Frames 1202-1232]

---

whom

1387

(*who, whom*) <u>*wrote*</u> *this story*

Because the verb *wrote* has no other subject, we choose

_____.

1388

No

1574

a. **We spoke to Mr. Fry. He owns the lot.**
b. **We spoke to Mr. Fry. The owner of the lot.**

Which arrangement is wrong because it contains a sentence fragment? ____

1575

---

asked

1761

We talked to the pilot, *and* we asked many questions.
We talked to the pilot *and* asked many questions.

Only one of these sentences requires a comma.

A comma is used only when the conjunction connects two (*sentences, verbs*).

1762

---

children's,
school's

1948

Lesson 68 Apostrophes for Missing Letters

[Frames 1950-1974]

Dorset Avenue,
Chinese

2135

The map shows you that minnesota extends farther north than maine or any other state. (2)

_____

2136

Parrots talk 73	Most sentences contain more than just two words. But no matter how long a sentence may be, it always contains a *subject* and a _____. 74
(shook) vigorously 261	Circle the verb and underline the adverb that modifies it: **Sandy leaves his toys everywhere.** 262
and, but 449	The word *compound* means "having two or more parts." **Wendy and Stan washed the dishes.** When the same verb has two or more subjects, we say that the subject is *com*_____. 450

sang, swam,
began
 	
637
	SIMPLE PAST: r<u>a</u>ng s<u>a</u>ng sw<u>a</u>m dr<u>a</u>nk beg<u>a</u>n
	PAST WITH HELPER:
	           (have) r<u>u</u>ng (have) s<u>u</u>ng (have) sw<u>u</u>m
	           (have) dr<u>u</u>nk (have) beg<u>u</u>n
	Do we use the same form of these verbs for the simple past and for the past with helper? (*Yes, No*)
	
	638

No 825	We needed to change the verb to make it agree with its subject only when it showed (*present, past*) time. 826
Yes 1013	**look feel taste smell** Each of these verbs, then, can be used as either an *action* verb or a _____ *ing* verb. 1014

DUPLICATING THE SUBJECT

A pronoun is used *in place of* a noun.

> a. **Laura looked in her mirror.**
> b. **She looked in her mirror.**

In which sentence is the subject a pronoun? ____

1202

---

who

(who, whom) the <u>police</u> <u>arrested</u>

Because the verb *arrested* already has a subject, we choose _____.

1388

1389

---

b

In this and the following frames, you will find two separate word groups. If both word groups are separate sentences, write *Correct* on the blank line.

EXAMPLE: **We fished all morning. We didn't catch a single fish.**

____*Correct*____ *(Turn to the next frame.)*

1575

1576

---

sentences

a. **The** <u>batter</u> <u>swung</u> **at the ball three times** *but* <u>**he**</u> **never even** <u>came</u> **close to it.**
b. **The** <u>batter</u> <u>swung</u> **at the ball three times** *but* **never even** <u>came</u> **close to it.**

In which sentence should you put a comma before the conjunction *but*? ____

1762

1763

In addition to showing ownership, the apostrophe is used to show where letters have been omitted from words.

> a. **The** *boys'* **mothers are invited.**
> b. **This window** *doesn't* **open.**

The apostrophe does not show ownership in sentence ____.

1950

Minnesota, Maine

Moslems, jews, and christians all consider jerusalem a holy city. (3)

_____

2136

2137

verb 74	All the words with which we build up a sentence are attached to either the subject or the verb. *A handsome, tall* **boy spoke.** In this sentence, the added italicized words go with the (*subject, verb*). 75
(leaves) everywhere 262	Circle the verb and underline the adverb that modifies it: **Often he skipped his breakfast.** 263
compound 450	When the same subject has two or more verbs, we say that the verb is *compound*. a. **Our dog ran away but returned.** b. **Our dog and cat ran away.** Which sentence contains a compound verb? ____ 451
No 638	SIMPLE PAST: r**a**ng s**a**ng sw**a**m dr**a**nk beg**a**n PAST WITH HELPER: (have) r**u**ng (have) s**u**ng (have) sw**u**m (have) dr**u**nk (have) beg**u**n When we change these verbs from simple past to past with helper, the *a* in each verb changes to ____. 639
present 826	Generally, there is no problem of subject-verb agreement when we use *simple past* verbs. The only exception is the simple past of the verb **be**—*was* and *were*. a. **The story was interesting.** b. **The stories were interesting.** The verb **was** is singular; the verb _____ is plural. 827
linking 1014	**look feel taste smell hear** Suppose that you use one of these verbs as an action verb. To tell *how* the action was performed, you would use an (*adjective, adverb*). 1015

b 1202	WRONG: **Laura** *she* **looked in her mirror.** The noun **Laura** makes it clear whom the sentence is about. Does the pronoun *she* serve any useful purpose? (*Yes, No*) 1203
whom 1389	Underline the correct clause signal: (*who, whom*) *guard* the President 1390
  1576	If one word group is a fragment, connect the two word groups by writing the last word of the first word group and the first word of the second word group with a small letter. EXAMPLE: **We fished all morning. Without catching a single fish.** *morning without* (*Turn to the next frame.*) 1577
a 1763	a. **Eleanor can write the invitations** *or* **help with the decorations.** b. **Eleanor can write the invitations** *or* **she can help with the decorations.** In which sentence should you put a comma before the conjunction *or*? ____ 1764
b 1950	As a shortcut, we often omit one or more letters from certain words. Then we attach the shortened word to another word, thus making a two-in-one word. **does not** *becomes* **doesn't** In **doesn't,** the apostrophe takes the place of the missing letter ____. 1951
Jews, Christians, Jerusalem 2137	**The Sahara desert extends from the Atlantic ocean to the Red sea. (3)** _____ 2138

Jack spoke *enthusiastically about his trip.*

In this sentence, the added italicized words go with the (*subject, verb*).

subject

75

76

---

often (skipped)

Circle the verb and underline the adverb that modifies it:

Leroy carried the baby clumsily.

263

264

---

a

Any basic part of a sentence can be compound: the subject, verb, direct object, or subject complement.

    a. **I washed my hands.**
    b. **I washed my hands and face.**

Which sentence contains a compound direct object? _____

451

452

---

u

    a. **rang**   **sang**   **swam**   **drank**   **began**
    b. **rung**   **sung**   **swum**   **drunk**   **begun**

Which words would you use after forms of the helping verbs **have** and **be**? _____

639

640

---

were

We say, "I *was* invited," but we say, "We _____ invited."

827

828

---

adverb

    look   **feel**   **taste**   **smell**   **sound**

Now suppose that you use one of these verbs as a linking verb.
The subject complement that follows it and describes the subject would need to be an (*adjective, adverb*).

1015

1016

No

Don't duplicate the subject by using both a noun and a pronoun to refer to the same person or thing. Use either the noun or the pronoun—not both.

    a. **Chuck he struck out.**   b. **Chuck struck out.**

Which one is wrong because it duplicates the subject? _____

1203

1204

---

who

Underline the correct clause signal:

    (who, whom) the President appointed

1390

1391

Now continue for yourself:

The headlights were too bright. They blinded the other driver.

_____

1577

1578

---

b

The acrobat missed the rope, and *he* **fell into the net.**

If you dropped the word *he,* would you still keep the comma? *(Yes, No)*

1764

1765

-o

To contract means "to get shorter." It is the opposite of the verb *to expand.* For this reason, we call these shortened words **contractions.**

    a. **we're**   b. **we are**

Which example is a *contraction?* _____

1951

1952

Desert, Ocean, Sea

Words in the english language are more difficult to spell than words in spanish or most other languages. (2)

_____

2138

2139

verb	**Jimmy looked** *enviously at my strawberry shortcake.* In this sentence, the added italicized words go with the (*subject, verb*).
76	77

(carried) <u>clumsily</u>	Now we shall do something else: **The fire engines arrived . .?. . (How?)** Underline the adverb that you could add to answer the question in parentheses: **here later fast soon**
264	265

b	**a. At first the dog was nervous.** **b. At first the dog was nervous and timid.** Which sentence contains a compound subject complement? ___
452	453

b	**ring sing swim drink begin** Whenever you use one of these words after any form of **have (has, had)** or **be (is, am, are—was, were, been).** you should change the *i* to (*a, u*).
640	641

were	We say, "The egg *was* fresh," but we say, "The eggs ___ fresh."
828	829

adjective	**a. The cloth** *felt* **rough.** **b. Judy** *felt* **the cloth roughly.** In one sentence, *felt* is an action verb; in the other, *felt* is a linking verb. In which one does *felt* mean an action of the hands? ___
1016	1017

a 1204	**This dog it wouldn't bite anybody.** Since **This dog** is the subject of the sentence, the pronoun _____ should be omitted. 1205
whom 1391	*whom the President appointed* We use the object form *whom* because the verb *appointed* already has a subject. The subject of the verb *appointed* is _____. 1392
Correct 1578	**Harold bought all the parts. And built the set himself.** _____ 1579
No 1765	a. **I set the alarm, but forgot to wind the clock.** b. **I set the alarm, but I forgot to wind the clock.** In which sentence is the comma used correctly? ____ 1766
a 1952	In a *contraction*, the apostrophe shows where one or more letters have been omitted. **we're** *means* **we are** In the contraction **we're**, the apostrophe takes the place of the missing letter ____. 1953
English, Spanish 2139	**A man with an irish terrier walks through woodside park every afternoon. (3)** _____ 2140

verb 77	*The thin paper* **bag tore.** In this sentence, the added italicized words go with the (*subject, verb*). 78
fast 265	**Henry waited .?. for his friends. (Where?)** Underline the adverb that would answer the question in parentheses: **eagerly often impatiently there** 266
b 453	Besides connecting words, the conjunctions **and, but,** and **or** can also connect two sentences into a single sentence. a. **My friend came over, and we worked on math.** b. **My friend came over and helped me with math.** The conjunction **and** connects two sentences in _____. 454
u 641	a. **The tardy bell** *has rang.* b. **The tardy bell** *has rung.* Which sentence is correct? _____ 642
were 829	**Vicky was late.** If we changed the subject to **Vicky and her sister**, we would change the singular verb **was** to the plural verb _____. 830
b 1017	**Judy** *felt* **the cloth roughly.** In this sentence, the verb *felt* means an action of the hands. To describe this action, we use the (*adjective, adverb*) **roughly.** 1018

it

1205

ORDER OF COURTESY

A courteous person serves others first and allows others to pass through a door ahead of him. It is also good manners to mention others first and yourself last.

a. **I and Carl stayed home.**   b. **Carl and I stayed home.**

Which sentence shows better manners? _____

1206

President

1392

Underline the correct clause signal:

(*who, whom*) *invented the electric light*

1393

---

parts and

1579

After Doris swallowed the pill. She read the label on the bottle.

_____

1580

---

b

1766

---

a. **The plane ran out of gas, and landed on a golf course.**
b. **The plane ran out of gas, and it landed on a golf course.**

From which sentence should the comma be dropped? _____

1767

---

a

1953

---

we'll *means* **we will**

In the contraction **we'll**, the apostrophe takes the place of the two missing letters _____.

1954

Irish,
Woodside Park

2140

There is a lutheran college on hickory lake in Milford county. (4)

_____

2141

subject 78	Underline the action verb with two lines: **<u>Frank</u> <u><u>left</u></u> in a great hurry.** 79
there 266	**I mow the lawn . ? . . (When?)** Underline the adverb that would answer the question in parentheses: **hastily willingly early usually** 267
a 454	a. **<u>We</u> <u><u>looked</u></u> for Dave, but <u>Dave</u> <u><u>had gone</u></u> home.** b. **<u>We</u> <u><u>looked</u></u> for Dave but <u><u>could</u></u> not <u><u>find</u></u> him.** In which sentence does the conjunction **but** connect two sentences? ____ 455
b 642	a. **We** *had* **just** *sang* **our school song.** b. **We** *had* **just** *sung* **our school song.** Which sentence is correct? ____ 643
were 830	a. **A few sandwiches . . . left over.** b. **One sandwich . . . left over.** In which sentence would **were** be correct? ____ 831
adverb 1018	**The cloth** *felt* **rough.** In this sentence, *felt* is a linking verb. It connects the adjective **rough** with the subject _____. 1019

b	a. **Chris played against me and her.** b. **Chris played against her and me.** Which sentence shows better manners? ____
1206	1207

who	Underline the correct clause signal: *(who, whom) the voters trust*
1393	1394

pill, she	**Steve sprained his wrist. The coach put Art into the game.** _____
1580	1581

a	The comma may be omitted when a compound sentence is short. a. **We visit them, and they visit us.** b. **We visit them during the Christmas holiday, and they visit us every summer.** From which sentence might you omit the comma? ____
1767	1768

wi	**I'd** *means* **I would** In the contraction **I'd**, the apostrophe takes the place of the four missing letters _____.
1954	1955

Lutheran, Hickory Lake, County	**The Suez canal shortens the distance between the United states and the Indian ocean by more than 6,000 miles. (3)** _____
2141	2142

left (underlined twice)	Underline the subject with one line: **The shaky old chair finally <u>collapsed</u>.**
79	80

early	**Paul .?. postponed his visit to the dentist. (How often?)** Underline the adverb that would answer the question in parentheses: **sometimes foolishly finally recently**
267	268

a	a. **You <u>can go</u> alone or <u>come</u> with us.** b. **You <u>can go</u> alone, or we <u>can pick</u> you up.** In which sentence does the conjunction **or** connect two sentences? ___
455	456

b	**We *swam* in that lake many times.** If you added the helper *have* to the verb, you would need to change *swam* to _____.
643	644

a	In English, the pronoun **you** always requires a plural verb. Always say, "You *were* . . ." even though you are speaking to one person. **You *were* in your room.** Would this sentence be correct if you were speaking to only one person? (*Yes, No*)
831	832

cloth	In this and the following frames, underline the correct modifier. If the verb shows action, choose the adverb. Otherwise, choose the adjective. **The cashier looked (*suspicious, suspiciously*) at the check.**
1019	1020

b 1207	a. **Miss Dale's class and we are putting on a play.** b. **We and Miss Dale's class are putting on a play.** Which sentence shows better manners? _____ 1208
whom 1394	In this and the following frames, write *who* or *whom,* depending on whether or not the clause signal is the subject of the clause. **The chairman** _____ *ran the meeting* **was capable.** 1395
Correct 1581	**I spent an hour in the library. Looking up material about occupations.** _____ 1582
a 1768	In this and the following frames, add a comma wherever the conjunction **and, but,** or **or** connects the two parts of a compound sentence. If the sentence is not compound, make no change. **The equipment was expensive and we lacked the money to buy it.** 1769
woul 1955	Do you know how to spell all the following contractions? it's (it i̶s) you've (you h̶ave) we'd (we w̶o̶u̶ld) let's (let u̶s) they're (they a̶re) there's (there i̶s) In which contraction does the apostrophe take the place of the largest number of letters? _____ 1956
Canal, States, Ocean 2142	Lesson **75** Capitals for Organizations and Institutions *page 160* [Frames 2144-2172]

chair 80	Underline the subject with one line and the verb with two lines: **The blue lake sparkled in the sun.** 81
sometimes 268	**They moved the furniture .?. . (How much?)** Underline the adverb that would answer the question in parentheses: **today slightly back carelessly** 269
b 456	A sentence made by connecting two or more simple sentences with the conjunction **and, but,** or **or** is a **compound sentence.** A sentence is not compound unless it has a subject and a verb both *before* and *after* the conjunction. **The crowd <u>stood</u> patiently *and* <u>waited</u> in the rain.** Is this sentence compound? (*Yes, No*) 457
swum 644	**Wendy *drank* all her milk.** If you added the helper *has* to the verb, you would need to change *drank* to _____. 645
Yes 832	Underline the correct verb: **You (*was, were*) the one who wanted to go.** 833
suspiciously 1020	**The check looked (*suspicious, suspiciously*) to the cashier.** 1021

"WE BOYS" AND "US GIRLS"

Some people do not know whether to use **we** or **us** in expressions like "we boys" and "us girls."

(*We, Us*) **boys can paint the fence.**

If you omitted the noun **boys,** which pronoun would you use? _____

1209

---

who

1395

The chairman _____ *we elect* **should be capable.**

1396

---

library, looking

1582

Aunt Jane served tapioca pudding. Which my dad doesn't like.

_____

1583

---

expensive, and

1769

Diane dived off the raft and swam to the boat.

1770

---

we'd

1956

The contraction of **it is** is _____.

The contraction of **you have** is _____.

1957

Capitalize the complete names of particular companies, stores, buildings, hotels, theaters, and so forth.

Ohio Oil Company   **Chrysler Building**   **Wayside Hotel**
Turner Garage   **Melody Record Shop**   **Capitol Theater**

Are words such as **company, building, hotel,** and **theater** capitalized when they are parts of names? (*Yes, No*)

2144

lake sparkled 81	A sentence is built around a _____ and a _____. 82
slightly 269	You can often turn an adjective into an adverb by adding **–ly** to it. **proud—proudly polite—politely timid—timidly serious—seriously** The adverb is the (*first, second*) word in each pair. 270
No 457	a. **The boys pushed hard and moved the rock.** b. **The boys pushed hard, and the rock moved.** Which sentence is compound? ____ 458
drunk 645	**The game** *began* **to get very exciting.** If you added the helper *had* to the verb, you would need to change *began* to _____. 646
were 833	When you use **was** or **were** to ask a question, look ahead to see whether the subject is singular or plural. a. ...**your dad at home?** b. ...**your parents at home?** In which sentence would it be a mistake to use the singu- lar verb **Was?** ____ 834
suspicious 1021	**The house smelled** (*musty, mustily*) **until we opened the window.** 1022

We 1209	**Our neighbor drove** (*we, us*) **girls to school.** If you omitted the noun **girls**, which pronoun would you use? _____ 1210
whom 1396	**Dr. Gaylord is a man** _____ *everyone admires.* 1397
pudding, which 1583	**Basketball takes brains. You have to make quick decisions.** _____ 1584
No comma 1770	**The mountain looks very close but it is over twenty miles away.** 1771
it's you've 1957	The contraction of **let us** is _____. The contraction of **there is** is _____. 1958
Yes 2144	a. **Terry works for the Beacon drug company.** b. **Terry works for the Beacon Drug Company.** Which sentence is correct? ____ 2145

subject, verb 82	The verb says something about the _____ of the sentence. 83
second 270	The adverb form of the adjective *clever* is _____. 271
b 458	**We waved and shouted at the passing ship.** Are there both a subject and a verb after the conjunction **and?** (*Yes, No*) 459
begun 646	**I had *drunk* too much ice water.** If you dropped the helper *had,* you would need to change the verb *drunk* to _____. 647
b 834	Underline the correct verb: (*Was, Were*) **your keys in that drawer?** 835
musty 1022	**Mother felt** (*unhappy, unhappily*) **about the scratch on the new table.** 1023

us	When you use expressions like "we boys" or "us girls," use the same pronoun you would use if the word *boys* or *girls* were omitted. Underline the correct pronoun: **Only two of** (*we, us*) ~~boys~~ **got a chance to play.**
1210	1211

whom	**Dr. Gaylord is a man** _____ *lives to help others.*
1397	1398

Correct	**Lois was walking with her dog. A black cocker spaniel.** _____
1584	1585

close, but	**You should visit Marjorie or send her a "get well" card.**
1771	1772

let's there's	The contraction of **they are** is _____. The contraction of **we would** is _____.
1958	1959

b	a. **My dad's office is in the Citizens' Bank Building.** b. **My dad's office is in the Citizens' bank building.** Which sentence is correct? ____
2145	2146

subject 83	Most verbs are action words. Verbs like *write, speak, bring,* and *carry* indicate actions of the (*mind, body*). 84
cleverly 271	The adverb form of the adjective *slight* is _____. 272
No 459	**We waved and shouted at the passing ship.** Is this a compound sentence? (*Yes, No*) 460
drank 647	**Our pitcher** *had begun* **to lose control.** If you dropped the helper *had,* you would need to change the verb *begun* to _____. 648
Were 835	In this and the following frames, underline the verb that agrees with its subject: **Our seats** (*were, was*) **close together.** 836
unhappy 1023	**This chocolate pie tastes** (*delicious, deliciously*). 1024

us 1211	Underline the correct pronoun: (*We, Us*) ~~girls~~ can meet at our house. 1212
who 1398	This story was written by an author _____ *understands* children. 1399
dog, a 1585	The party was a success. Everyone had a good time. _____ 1586
No comma 1772	You must get up early or you will miss the sunrise. 1773
they're we'd 1959	Very many contractions are made by shortening the adverb *not* to *n't*. isn't doesn't aren't haven't In each of these contractions, the apostrophe takes the place of the missing letter ____. 1960
a 2146	The ʌ theater will open next week. If you inserted the name **Rosedale** before the noun **theater**, would you capitalize the noun **theater**? (*Yes, No*) 2147

body	Verbs like *decide, worry, want,* and *expect* indicate actions of the (*mind, body*).
84	85

slightly	Underline the adverb: **A foolish person talks foolishly.**
272	273

No	If a sentence is compound, you can break it into two separate sentences, each with a subject and a verb. a. **My eyes were closed, but I wasn't sleeping.** b. **I closed my eyes and pretended to be asleep.** Which sentence is compound? ____
460	461

began	Remember that after all forms of **be (is, am, are—was, were, been),** you must also use the helper form. a. **The tardy bell** *was rang* **too early.** b. **The tardy bell** *was rung* **too early.** Which sentence is correct? ____
648	649

were	**Ricky** (*don't, doesn't*) **waste his money.**
836	837

delicious	**We could smell gas very** (*distinct, distinctly*) **in the kitchen.**
1024	1025

We

Underline the correct pronoun:

Some of (*we*, *us*) students did not see the notice.

---

who

Don't accept a ride from anyone _____ *you don't know*.

Correct

Our dog Jiggs feels hurt. When we don't pay attention to him.

_____

---

early, or

A dachshund's body is long and its legs are very short.

---

o

People sometimes forget that the apostrophe takes the place of the missing **o** in such words as **isn't** and **doesn't**. As a result, they put the apostrophe in the wrong place.

    a. **wasn't**   **aren't**   **hasn't**   **doesn't**
    b. **was'nt**   **are'nt**   **has'nt**   **does'nt**

In which group are the contractions spelled correctly? ____

Yes

The Dorset Hotel is very modern.

If you dropped the name **Dorset,** would you still write **Hotel** with a capital letter? (*Yes, No*)

foolishly

273

a. **What kind? Which one(s)? How many?**
b. **When? Where? How? How often?**

Adverbs would answer the questions in group (*a, b*).

274

---

a

461

Put a comma before the conjunction **and, but,** or **or** that connects the two parts of a compound sentence.

a. **I looked in my drawer and found my wallet.**
b. **I looked in my drawer and my wallet was there.**

Which sentence is compound and therefore requires a comma before **and?** _____

462

---

b

649

a. **The songs** *were sang* **without accompaniment.**
b. **The songs** *were sung* **without accompaniment.**

Which sentence is correct? _____

650

---

doesn't

837

We (*were, was*) **just about to eat dinner.**

838

---

distinctly

1025

The color looks (*different, differently*) **in the daylight.**

1026

us 1213	(*Us, We*) eighth-graders will serve as ushers. 1214
whom 1400	When the clause signal is the subject of the clause, always choose (*who, whom*). 1401
hurt when 1587	**Suddenly Mother rushed to the kitchen. Remembering the cake in the oven.** _____ 1588
long, and 1774	**We tried every brand of dog food but Pepper wouldn't eat any of them.** 1775
a 1961	In all the **n't** words, remember to put the apostrophe in place of the missing **o.** The contraction of **are not** is _____. The contraction of **did not** is _____. 1962
No 2148	Capitalize the complete names of particular schools, colleges, churches, hospitals, libraries, and so forth. **Cody High School** **Bethel Church** **Franklin Library** **Albion College** **Dover Art Club** **Fremont Hospital** Are words such as **school, church, library,** and **hospital** capitalized when they are parts of names? (*Yes, No*) 2149

Verbs generally show by their spelling whether they mean *present* or *past* time.

> a. **We** *live* **in Texas.**
> b. **We** *lived* **in Texas.**

In which sentence does the verb show *present* time? ____

87

---

b

a. **always, never, recently, forever**
b. **here, there, away, aside, everywhere**
c. **steadily, happily, successfully, cheerfully**

All the above words can be used as adverbs. In which group would the words answer the question *How?* ____

274

275

---

b

a. **You can bring your own lunch, or buy it in the cafeteria.**
b. **I must get enough sleep, or I feel tired the next day.**

One of these sentences is not compound. A comma, therefore, should not be used.

The comma should be omitted in sentence ____.

462

463

---

b

Write the missing forms of these verbs:

PRESENT	SIMPLE PAST	PAST WITH HELPER
drink	drank	(have) _____
begin	began	(have) _____
swim	swam	(have) _____

650

651

---

were

This cover (*doesn't, don't*) **fit the jar.**

838

839

---

different

His plan sounded rather (*dishonest, dishonestly*) **to me.**

1026

1027

We 1214	Most of (*us*, *we*) boys attend every game. 1215
who 1401	Lesson **48** Using *Who*, *Which*, and *That* Correctly [Frames 1403-1421]
kitchen, remembering 1588	Lesson **55** Sentences That Forget to Stop [Frames 1590-1617]
food, but 1775	Many people must work at night and sleep during the day. 1776
aren't didn't 1962	**can't** *means* **cannot** In the contraction **can't**, the apostrophe takes the place of two missing letters: ____ and ____. 1963
Yes 2149	a. **I attend the Preston Junior High School.** b. **I attend the Preston junior high school.** Which sentence is correct? ____ 2150

a	a. We *take* several magazines. b. We *took* several magazines. In which sentences does the verb show *past* time? _____
87	88
c	Do you always find an adverb next to the word it modifies? (*Yes, No*)
275	276
a	The teacher paused at my desk, and *she* looked at my composition. If you omitted the subject *she* in the second part of the sentence, would the sentence still be compound? (*Yes, No*)
463	464
drunk begun swum	Write the correct past form of **ring**: The fire alarm had been _____ by mistake.
651	652
doesn't	My dad and my mother (*was, were*) in the living room.
839	840
dishonest	You can taste the lemon very (*definite, definitely*) in this cake.
1027	1028

THEM OR THOSE?

Never use the pronoun **them** to point something out. The proper word for pointing out is **those**.

> a. *Them* **are my books.**
> b. *Those* **are my books.**

Which sentence is correct? ____

us

1215

1216

CLAUSE SIGNALS: **who (whom, whose), which, that**

Use **who** and **whom** to refer to persons.
Use **which** to refer to things and animals.

Underline the correct clause signal:

The clerk (*who, which*) **waited on me was very patient.**

1403

A person who writes a sentence fragment mistakes a piece of a sentence for a complete sentence.

> a. **Knowing several people in this town.**
> b. **I knew several people in this town.**

Which is a sentence fragment? ____

1590

No comma

A package must be properly wrapped or the post office will not accept it.

1776

1777

One **n't** contraction is different from all the others:
won't (w~~ill~~ n~~o~~t)

There is the usual apostrophe to take the place of the missing **o** in **not**.

However, the letters **ill** in **will** disappear completely, and after the **w** we find the letter ____.

n, o

1963

1964

> a. **My brother just graduated from high school.**
> b. **My brother just graduated from Kirk high school.**

In which sentence should the words **high school** be capitalized because they are part of the name of a particular school? ____

a

2150

2151

b 88	When you change a sentence from present time to past time, or from past time to present time, the verb generally changes its spelling. PRESENT: **My friend usually** *rides* **to school.** If you changed this sentence to *past* time, you would need to change the verb *rides* to _____. 89
No 276	Many adverbs, especially those that tell *how,* end with the letters (*–tion, –ly, –ing*). 277
No 464	**The teacher paused at my desk, and** *she* **looked at my com-position.** If you omitted the subject *she* in the second part of the sentence, would you keep the comma before **and?** (*Yes, No*) 465
rung 652	Write the correct past form of **drink:** **Someone has _____ all my lemonade.** 653
were 840	**This tie and this shirt** (*don't, doesn't*) **match.** 841
definitely	Lesson **35** How to Make Comparisons

b 1216	The pronoun **them** is the object form of **they.** It should be used for direct objects and for objects of prepositions, not to point something out. a. **I left** *them* **at school.** b. *Them* **are not mine.** In which sentence is *them* used correctly? ____ <div style="text-align:right">1217</div>
who 1403	Remember: **who** and **whom**.........persons **which**.....................things and animals Underline the correct clause signal: **Our neighbors have a crow** (*who, which*) **can talk.** <div style="text-align:right">1404</div>
a 1590	Some people make the opposite error. They reach the end of a sentence and keep right on going into the next. First, let us look at two separate sentences: <u>We</u> <u>took</u> our seats. The <u>show</u> <u>began.</u> These are two separate sentences, each with a subject and a _____. <div style="text-align:right">1591</div>
wrapped, or 1777	Lesson **62** **Commas After Introductory Word Groups** [Frames 1779-1806]
o 1964	The contraction of **will not** is _____. <div style="text-align:right">1965</div>
b 2151	**a Methodist church** This is not the name of a *particular* church at a *particular* location. It could mean *any* Methodist church anywhere in the world. Is the word **church** capitalized? (*Yes, No*) <div style="text-align:right">2152</div>

rode

89

PAST: **The catcher** *stood* **behind the plate.**

If you changed this sentence to *present* time, you would

need to change the verb *stood* to _____.

90

–ly

277

Lesson **10** **Adverbs**
That Control the Power

[Frames 279-312]

No

465

Douglas kept his old friends and ∧ **made several new ones.**

If you added the subject **he** at the point indicated by the
caret (∧), would you add a comma before the conjunction
and? (*Yes, No*)

466

---

drunk

653

Write the correct past form of **begin:**

One of the engines had _____ to miss.

654

---

don't

841

Lesson **28** **Don't Let Phrases Fool You!**

[Frames 843-872]

A plane is *fast.*

In this sentence, do we compare a plane with any other
means of travel? (*Yes, No*)

1030

a	a. **Are** *them* **too big for me?** b. **I didn't look at** *them.* In which sentence is *them* used correctly? ____ 1218
which 1404	a. **Dan has a rifle ... is 100 years old.** b. **Dan has a great-uncle ... is 100 years old.** In which sentence would **which** be correct? ____ 1405
verb 1591	**We took our seats. The show began.** We show the end of a sentence by putting down an end mark—a period, a question mark, or an exclamation point. Then we start the next sentence with a _____ letter. 1592
	I saw an unusual sight *on my way to school.* This sentence consists of two word groups. The first word group tells *what happened.* The second word group tells only *where* it happened. The more important word group comes (*first, last*). 1779
won't 1965	In this and the following frames, write between the parentheses the correct contraction for each pair of italicized words. Remember that the apostrophe goes in where the letter or letters come out. *Let us* (_____) **see if** *it is* (_____) **ready.** 1966
No 2152	**Westport Methodist Church** This is the name of a *particular* Methodist church at a *particular* location. Is the word **church** capitalized? (*Yes, No*) 2153

stands

90

If you are doubtful about which word in a sentence is the verb, change the sentence from present to past time or from past to present time to see which word changes. The word that changes is the (*subject, verb*).

91

There are two kinds of words that modify other words. One kind is called *adjectives,* and the other kind is called

_____.

279

Yes

466

Compound means "having _____ or more parts." (How many?)

467

begun

654

Write the correct past form of each verb in parentheses:

The dismissal bell _____ (*ring*) before we had _____ (*sing*) our song.

655

One <u>was</u> very noisy.

The subject **One** is singular; the verb **was** is singular, too.

We say, therefore, that the subject and the verb _____ in number.

843

A plane is *faster* than a train.

When we compare a plane with *one* other means of travel,

we change the word *fast* to _____.

No

1030

1031

b 1218	Underline the correct word: 　　(*Them, Those*) **belong to our neighbor.** 　　　　　　　　　　　　　　　　　　　　　　　1219
a 1405	a. **Mr. Prentis has a pupil ... is always slow.** 　b. **Mr. Prentis has a watch ... is always slow.** In which sentence would **which** be correct? ____ 　　　　　　　　　　　　　　　　　　　　　　　1406
capital 1592	A period (or a question mark or an exclamation point) is a stop signal. It tells the reader that the sentence has ended. A comma tells the reader only to pause—that more of the sentence is coming. You know that a sentence ends when you see a (*comma, period*). 　　　　　　　　　　　　　　　　　　　　　　　1593
first 1779	a. **I saw an unusual sight**　　*on my way to school.* 　b. *On my way to school,*　　**I saw an unusual sight.** In which sentence does the modifying word group come before the main statement? ____ 　　　　　　　　　　　　　　　　　　　　　　　1780
Let's, it's 1966	**It** *does not* (_____) **seem to me that** *they are* (_____) **trying to win.** 　　　　　　　　　　　　　　　　　　　　　　　1967
Yes 2153	a. **a Methodist Church** 　b. **Westport Methodist Church** In which example is it a mistake to capitalize the word **church?** ____ 　　　　　　　　　　　　　　　　　　　　　　　2154

verb 91	Underline the verb with two lines: **<u>I</u> generally <u>see</u> my dentist twice a year.** 92
adverbs 279	Both adjectives and adverbs make the pictures and ideas we get from words (*more, less*) clear and exact. 280
two 467	Words that connect words or groups of words are called _____. 468
rang, sung 655	Write the correct past form of each verb in parentheses: **Before we had _____ (*swim*) across the stream, it _____ (*begin*) to rain.** 656
agree 843	**One <u>was</u> very noisy.** Do you know whether the subject **One** refers to a motor, a child, a record, or a room? (*Yes, No*) 844
faster 1031	**A plane is the *fastest* means of travel.** There are many means of travel—horses, cars, boats, buses, trains, and so forth. In this sentence, are we comparing a plane with *more than one* other means of travel? (*Yes, No*) 1032

Neither should you use **them** as an adjective to point out the noun that follows it.

Underline the correct word:

(*Those, Them*) **flowers belong to our neighbor.**

---

a. **This is the light ... directs the traffic.**
b. **This is the officer ... directs the traffic.**

In which sentence would **which** be correct? ____

When one sentence runs into another, the result is called a **run-on sentence.** It is a bad mistake in writing.

a. <u>We</u> <u>took</u> our seats. The <u>show</u> <u>began.</u>
b. <u>We</u> <u>took</u> our seats, the <u>show</u> <u>began.</u>

Which is a run-on sentence? ____

The word **introductory** means "leading into." An introductory paragraph leads into the story. An introductory remark leads into the speech. An introductory phrase or clause leads into the main statement.

An introductory word group comes (*before, after*) the main statement of a sentence.

I would (_____) **like to know if** *you are* (_____)
going to the game.

The St. Agnes Catholic *Church* **is not the only Catholic** *Church* **in our town.**

Because it is not part of the name of a *particular* church building, the (*first, second*) italicized word should not be capitalized.

Underline the verb with two lines:

The <u>boy</u> in the back seat knows all the answers.

93

---

more

280

We call a person who drives a *driver;* one who bakes, a *baker;* one who pitches, a *pitcher.* In the same way, we call a word that modifies another word a *modifier.*

Both adjectives and adverbs are _____.

281

---

conjunctions

468

The three most common conjunctions are the words

_____, _____, and _____.

469

---

swum, began

656

The verb **bring** looks very similar to **ring** and **sing**, but it behaves quite differently.

PRESENT	SIMPLE PAST	PAST WITH HELPER
bring	**brought**	**(have) brought**

Do we use the same past form of **bring** for both the simple past and for the past with helper? (*Yes, No*)

657

No

844

To make clear what **One** refers to, we shall add a prepositional phrase.

One *of the motors* **was very noisy.**

The prepositional phrase starts with the preposition _____

and ends with its object _____.

845

Yes

1032

A plane is the *fastest* means of travel.

When we compare a plane with *more than one* other

means of travel, we use the adjective _____.

1033

Those 1220	Underline the correct word: **I had never seen** (*those, them*) **boys before.** <div align="right">1221</div>
a 1407	Never use the clause signal **which** to refer to (*animals, persons, things*). <div align="right">1408</div>

b
 	
1594
	Sometimes a person runs one sentence into another with only a comma between them. Sometimes he runs them together with nothing between them. Both are equally wrong.
	
	    a. **We took our seats the show began.**
	    b. **We took our seats, the show began.**
	
	Are both *a* and *b* run-on sentences? (*Yes, No*)
	<div align="right">1595</div>

before 1781	a. **I saw an unusual sight** *on my way to school.* b. *On my way to school,* **I saw an unusual sight.** Which sentence begins with an introductory word group? _____ <div align="right">1782</div>
I'd, you're 1968	**Virginia** *cannot* (_____) **study well when** *there is* (_____) **too much noise.** <div align="right">1969</div>
second 2155	**We met at the Trinity Episcopal Church** If you dropped the name **Trinity**, would you still write **Church** with a capital letter? (*Yes, No*) <div align="right">2156</div>

<u>knows</u> 93	Underline the verb with two lines: **The first <u>chapter</u> described the ranch.** 94
modifiers 281	The modifiers that we use with nouns and pronouns are called _____. 282
and, but, or 469	In a compound sentence, put a comma (*before, after*) the conjunction **and, but,** or **or.** 470
Yes 657	PRESENT SIMPLE PAST PAST WITH HELPER **bring** **brought** **(have) brought** Write the correct past forms of **bring:** **Peggy** _____ **the same kind of cookies that Ann** **had** _____ **last week.** 658
of, motors 845	**One** *of the motors* **was very noisy.** The prepositional phrase *of the motors* modifies the subject of this sentence, which is the pronoun _____. 846
fastest 1033	**A plane is** *faster* **than a train.** **A plane is the** *fastest* **means of travel.** When we compare a plane with one other means of travel, we add _____ to the word *fast.* When we compare a plane with more than one other means of travel, we add _____ to the word *fast.* 1034

those 1221	Underline the correct word: **Why don't you put** (*them, those*) **stamps in your album?** 1222
persons 1408	driver nurse fireman doctor Would it be correct to use the clause signal **which** to refer to any of the above nouns? (*Yes, No*) 1409
Yes 1595	a. **We took our seats the show began.** b. **We took our seats, the show began.** Both *a* and *b* are run-on sentences. There is no _____ to show where the first sentence ends. There is no _____ letter to show where the second sentence begins. 1596
b 1782	a. **I saw an unusual sight** *on my way to school.* b. *On my way to school,* **I saw an unusual sight.** One sentence has a comma; the other does not. The comma is necessary only when the sentence begins with the (*main statement, introductory word group*). 1783
can't, there's 1969	*He will* (_____) **let you know if he** *is not* (_____) **satisfied.** 1970

No
 	
2156
	Capitalize the names of *particular* clubs and organizations.
	    a. **The Schubert music club will provide the orchestra.**
	    b. **A music club will provide the orchestra.**
	In which sentence should the words **music club** be capitalized because they are part of the name of a particular club? ____
	
	2157

described 94	To find the subject and verb in a sentence, it is better to find the verb first. Let's suppose that the verb is *told*. Now ask yourself, "Who or what *told?*" The answer to this question is always the subject. **The new boy from Alaska told about his trip.** Who **told?** _____ (one word) 95
adjectives 282	The modifiers that we use with verbs are called _____. 283
before 470	Lesson **16** Unit Review [Frames 472-503]
brought, brought 658	PRESENT SIMPLE PAST PAST WITH HELPER ring rang (have) rung sing sang (have) sung bring brought (have) brought Which of these three verbs behaves differently from the other two? _____ 659
One 846	**One** *of the motors* **was very noisy.** We have added a prepositional phrase merely to make clear what we mean by **One.** The subject of this sentence is still the word _____. 847
–er, –est 1034	Most adjectives and adverbs have three degrees (or steps) of power. The *first degree* merely states a quality—like *young, slow, clean.* Underline the adjective in the first degree: **fast faster fastest** *page 189* 1035

those 1222	In this and the following frames, underline the correct word or words, according to the rules you studied in this lesson: (*We, Us*) **boys can decorate the gym.** 1223

No
 	
1409
	The clause signal **that** can be used to refer to persons, things, or animals.
	
	    a. **I like people ... are jolly.**
	    b. **I like a room ... is cozy.**
	    c. **I like dogs ... obey promptly.**
	
	Would **that** be correct in each of these sentences? (*Yes, No*)
	
	1410

period capital 1596	You learned earlier how to join two sentences into a compound sentence. You merely put the conjunction (connecting word) **and, but,** or **or** between them. **We took our seats,** *and* **the show began.** The two sentences are joined by the conjunction _____. 1597
introductory word group 1783	The comma after an introductory word group helps you to read the sentence correctly. **While I was eating the cat jumped on my lap.** The reader might get the wrong meaning unless we put a comma after (*eating, cat*). 1784
He'll, isn't 1970	*She is* (_____) **very sure that Mickey** *has not* (_____) **written to him.** 1971
a 2157	Do not capitalize the word **the, and,** or any short preposition (**of, in, for, to**) when it is part of a name. **Society for the Prevention of Cruelty to Animals** How many words in this name are not capitalized? _____ 2158

The new boy from Alaska told about his trip.

The subject of the verb **told** is _____.

96

---

a high mountain

Because the word **high** modifies the noun **mountain,** it is an

_____.

284

Certain words answer the questions *What kind? Which one*(s)? *How many?* and *How much?* about nouns and pronouns.

These words are called _____.

472

Write the correct past form of each verb in parentheses:

We _____ (*sing*) **songs from books that Miss Roth had**

_____ (*bring*) **to the meeting.**

660

One *of the motors* **was very noisy.**

The singular pronoun **One** is the subject of this sentence.

In choosing our verb, should we pay any attention to the plural noun *motors? (Yes, No)*

848

The *second degree* shows that one of *two* things has *more* of this quality than the other—*younger, slower, cleaner.* Underline the adjective in the second degree:

fast   faster   fastest

1036

We

1223

(*Our teacher, Our teacher she*) **goes to all the games.**

1224

Yes

1410

---

a. **People** *who* **are lazy find excuses.**
b. **The suit** *which* **he wore needed pressing.**

Could you use **that** in place of the italicized clause signal in each sentence? (*Yes, No*)

1411

---

and

1597

---

a. **We took our seats, the show began.**
b. **We took our seats, and the show began.**

Which is wrong because it is a run-on sentence? _____

1598

---

eating

1784

Put a comma after an introductory word group—a word group that comes ahead of the main statement.

a. **At the end of the game   we cheered the other team.**
b. **We cheered the other team   at the end of the game.**

Which sentence requires a comma? _____

1785

She's, hasn't

1971

You *have not* (_____) **told Phyllis that** *we are*

(_____) **going to the carnival.**

1972

---

four

2158

Here is the name of a national organization. Underline two words that should not be capitalized:

national conference of christians and jews

2159

boy 96	**Apples from our neighbors' tree fell into our yard.** What **fell?** _____ (one word) 97

adjective
 	
284
	All mountains are high, but some are much higher than others.
	
	      a. **a high mountain**
	      b. **a very high mountain**
	
	Which gives you the idea of a higher mountain—*a* or *b*? ___
	
	285

adjectives 472	Underline three adjectives in this sentence: **Good seats for this concert cost two dollars.** 473
sang, brought 660	Write the correct past form of each verb in parentheses: **The bell had** _____ (*ring*) **before Dave** _____ (*bring*) **back the report from the office.** 661
No 848	**One ... the flute.** **One of my sisters ... the flute.** Would the singular verb **plays** be correct in both sentences? (*Yes, No*) 849
faster 1036	The *third degree* shows that one of *three or more* things has the *most* of this quality—*youngest, slowest, cleanest.* Underline the adjective in the third degree: **fast faster fastest** 1037

Our teacher 1224	Grandfather fascinated (*we, us*) children with stories of his adventures. 1225
Yes 1411	We feed a squirrel . . . comes to our door. The *two* clause signals that would be correct in this sentence are (*who, which, that*). 1412
a 1598	Is it correct to separate two sentences by putting only a comma between them? (*Yes, No*) 1599
a 1785	Bears can run fast although they look slow and clumsy. Suppose that you saw a bear close to you in the woods. The more important fact for you to know is in the (*first, second*) word group. 1786
haven't, we're 1972	You *should not* (_____) buy it just because *it is* (_____) cheap. 1973
of, and 2159	Underline two words that should not be capitalized: **american foundation for the blind** 2160

Apples	**Apples from our neighbors' tree fell into our yard.** The subject of the verb **fell** is _____.
97	98

b	a. **a high mountain** b. **a very high mountain** The words after *b* give you an idea of greater height because the word _____ has been added.
285	286

good, this, two	Some words can be used as either nouns or adjectives, depending on the job they do in the sentence. a. **I prefer** *light* **colors.** b. **The** *light* **went out.** In which sentence is *light* used as an adjective? _____
473	474

rung, brought	Lesson **22** Straightening Out *Lie* and *Lay* [Frames 663-695]
661	

Yes	a. **My sisters ... the flute.** b. **One of my sisters ... the flute.** In which sentence would the plural verb **play** be correct because the subject is plural? _____
849	850

	FIRST DEGREE	SECOND DEGREE	THIRD DEGREE

	FIRST DEGREE	SECOND DEGREE	THIRD DEGREE
	high	**high<u>er</u>**	**high<u>est</u>**
fastest	**strong**	**strong<u>er</u>**	**strong<u>est</u>**

With short words of one syllable (and sometimes two) we form the second degree by adding *–er;* the third degree by adding _____.

1037	1038

us 1225	Mr. Page let (*me and Phyllis, Phyllis and me*) **use his canoe.** 1226

which, that
 	
1412
	In this and the following frames, underline the correct clause signal.
	
	Remember: **who** and **whom**...persons
	           which ....things and animals
	           that ....persons, things, and animals
	
	        any bank (*which, who*)
	1413

No 1599	A comma is often right when one of the two word groups is *not* a sentence. *When we took our seats,* **the show began.** Is this a run-on sentence? (*Yes, No*) 1600
first 1786	a. **Bears can run fast** **although they look slow and clumsy.** b. **Although they look slow and clumsy** **bears can run fast.** Which sentence begins with an introductory word group, not with the main statement? ____ 1787
shouldn't, it's 1973	**The elevator** *will not* (_____) **start if the doors** *are* *not* (_____) **closed.** 1974
for, the 2160	**My best friend is in the** ∧ **hospital.** If you inserted the name **Lancaster** before the noun **hospital,** would you capitalize the noun **hospital?** (*Yes, No*) 2161

Apples 98	In most sentences that state a fact, the subject comes *before* the verb, not *after* it. **People often <u>complain</u> about the weather.** The subject of the verb **complain** is (*People, weather*). <div align="right">99</div>
very 286	**a *very* high mountain** The word *very* modifies the adjective **high**. It tells _____ **high** the mountain is. <div align="right">287</div>
a 474	a. **The *glass* broke.** b. **We used a *glass* pitcher.** In which sentence is *glass* used as an adjective? ____ <div align="right">475</div>
	To lie means "to rest in a flat position" or "to be in place." We say, "I *lie* in bed and read" and "The rug *lies* on the floor." Supply the missing word: **Our cat often _____ on the windowsill.** <div align="right">663</div>
a 850	Don't let a prepositional phrase that follows the subject trick you into choosing the wrong verb. Here are nine common prepositions that often start such phrases: PREPOSITIONS: **of in to at on by for from with** **The need *for more schools* (is, are) very great.** The subject of this sentence is (*need, schools*). <div align="right">851</div>
–est 1038	The second degree of *cheap* is _____. The third degree of *cheap* is _____. <div align="right">1039</div>

Phyllis and me

1226

(*Those, Them*) **are exactly like ours.**

1227

---

which

1413

the teacher (*which, that*)

1414

No

1600

a. **I turned off the light, I went to sleep.**
b. **Turning off the light, I went to sleep.**

Which is a run-on sentence? ____

1601

---

b

1787

Although they look clumsy, bears can run fast.

We use a comma in this sentence because it begins with the (*main statement, introductory word group*).

1788

---

won't, aren't

1974

Lesson **69** Possessive Pronouns—
No Apostrophes!

[Frames 1976-1997]

Yes

2161

a. **My aunt is a nurse at the Hospital.**
b. **My aunt is a nurse at the Redstone County Hospital.**

Which sentence is correct? ____

2162

People 99	**The bright lights <u>blinded</u> the driver.** The subject of the verb **blinded** is (*lights, driver*). 100
how 287	**drove slowly** Because the word **slowly** modifies the verb **drove**, it is an _____. 288
b 475	Certain words answer the questions *When? Where? How? How much?* and *How often?* about the actions of verbs. These words are called _____. 476
lies 663	PRESENT SIMPLE PAST PAST WITH HELPER **lie** (in bed) **lay** **(have) lain** Is the word **laid** either one of the past forms of the verb **lie?** (*Yes, No*) 664
need 851	Underline the verb that agrees with the subject: **The need for more schools** (*is, are*) **very great.** 852
cheaper cheapest 1039	To compare one person or thing with another person or thing, we use the second degree, which ends with the letters (*–er, –est*). 1040

Those 1227	**This book** (*it's, is*) **about cowboys.** 1228
that 1414	**the mouse** (*who, which*) 1415
a 1601	a. **The wrappers are different. The candy is all alike.** b. **Although the wrappers are different, the candy is all alike.** c. **The wrappers are different, the candy is all alike.** Which is a run-on sentence? ____ 1602
introductory word group 1788	a. **After I returned to the city my coat of tan soon faded.** b. **My coat of tan soon faded after I returned to the city.** Which sentence requires a comma? ____ 1789
	To possess means "to own." A family may possess, or own, their own home. Pronouns that show ownership are called **possessive** pronouns. **mine yours his hers its ours theirs** Do you see an apostrophe before the final *s* in any of these possessive pronouns? (*Yes, No*) 1976
b 2162	a. **You can get the book at the Emerson library.** b. **You can get the book at almost any library.** In which sentence should **library** be capitalized? ____ 2163

lights 100	In this and the following frames, find the verb first and underline it with two lines. Then use the *Who?—What?* method to find the subject and underline it with one line. **The meeting started on time.** 101

adverb
 	
288
	The word **slowly** could mean anything from scarcely moving to perhaps fifteen or twenty miles per hour.
	
	    a. **drove slowly**
	    b. **drove very slowly.**
	
	Which gives you the idea of slower speed—*a* or *b*? ____
	
	289

adverbs 476	Underline two adverbs in this sentence: **There he waited patiently for his friend.** 477
No 664	PRESENT SIMPLE PAST PAST WITH HELPER **lie** (in bed) **lay** **(have) lain** The simple past form of **lie** is not **laid** but _____. 665
is 852	**The pictures on the wall (show, shows) the history of our country.** The subject of this sentence is (*pictures, wall*). 853
–er 1040	Underline the correct adjective: **Paul is the (*shorter, shortest*) of the two boys.** 1041

is 1228	(*We, Us*) girls must stick together in this election. 1229
which 1415	**the cashier** (*that, which*) 1416
c 1602	Beginning in the next frame, you will find a story about the adventure of a truck driver. If the sentence is correct, write *Correct* on the blank line. If the sentence is a run-on sentence, correct it like this: EXAMPLE: **The soup was too salty, nobody could eat it.** *salty. Nobody* (*Turn to the next frame.*) 1603
a 1789	a. **As we were rowing toward shore we noticed a black cloud.** b. **We noticed a black cloud as we were rowing toward shore.** Which sentence requires a comma? ____ 1790
No 1976	To make nouns show ownership, we need to use apostrophes. *John's* **score was higher than** *Helen's* **score.** In this sentence, there are two nouns that show ownership. Are both these nouns written with apostrophes? (*Yes, No*) 1977
a 2163	In this and the following frames, copy and capitalize only the words to which capitals should be added: **When I complete high school, I plan to go to Cornell university.** 2164

meeting started	Continue to underline the verb with two lines and the subject with one.
	Huge waves crashed noisily against the rocks.
101	102

	a. **drove slowly**
	b. **drove very slowly**
b	The words after *b* give you the idea of slower speed because the word _____ has been added.
289	290

	Some words can be used as either adjectives or adverbs, depending on whether they modify nouns (pronouns) or verbs.
	a. **The band played** *loud.*
There, patiently	b. **Perry has a** *loud* **voice.**
	In which sentence is *loud* used as an adverb? ____
477	478

	Underline the correct verb:
lay	**Last night I** *(lay, laid)* **on the sofa and watched television.**
665	666

	Underline the verb that agrees with the subject:
pictures	**The pictures on the wall** *(show, shows)* **the history of our country.**
853	854

	When our comparison involves three or more persons or things, we use the third degree, which ends with the letters *(-er, -est)*.
shorter	
1041	1042

We

1229

How much is one of (*those, them*) **apples?**

1230

---

that

1416

---

libraries (*who, that*)

1417

As Joe Kelly was driving his truck out Main Street, he heard a siren.

_____

1603

1604

---

a

1790

When they have nothing to do, **children often quarrel.**

If you moved the introductory clause to the end of the sentence, would you use a comma in this sentence? (*Yes, No*)

1791

Yes

1977

Possessive pronouns are different from nouns. They are possessive words in themselves. They show ownership without the use of apostrophes.

Yours **was higher than** *hers.*

Here we have two pronouns that show ownership.

Is either pronoun written with an apostrophe? (*Yes, No*)

1978

University

2164

The Parkman library circulates books among the patients at Auburn children's hospital.

_____

2165

waves crashed 102	**An old British fort once stood on this spot.** 103
very 290	**drove** *very* **slowly** The word *very* tells how **slowly** someone drove. The word *very*, therefore, modifies the adverb _____. 291
a 478	a. **He took a** *fast* **train.** b. **He talks** *fast.* In which sentence is *fast* used as an adverb? _____ 479
lay 666	Underline the correct verb: **Heavy clouds** (*laid, lay*) **over the airport all day.** 667
show 854	Here are two groups of words that you might make sentences about. Underline the word in each group with which the verb would need to agree: a. **My interest in rocks...** b. **The visitors from Philadelphia...** 855
–est 1042	Underline the correct modifier: **Paul is the** (*shorter, shortest*) **of the three boys.** 1043

those 1230	(*We and our neighbors, Our neighbors and we*) **cleaned up the vacant lot.** 1231
that 1417	**a dentist** (*who, which*) 1418
Correct 1604	**A moment later he looked back, a fire engine was just behind him.** _____ 1605
No 1791	**The Mississippi River became a busy waterway** *after the steamboat was invented.* If you moved the italicized clause to the beginning of the sentence, would you put a comma after it? (*Yes, No*) 1792
No 1978	You are in the habit of using apostrophes in possessive nouns. Therefore, you must make a special effort not to use apostrophes whenever you write possessive pronouns. Add *one* apostrophe to this sentence: *Bobs* **locker is right next to** *ours.* 1979
Library, Children's Hospital 2165	**We were taken by bus from our hotel to the empire state building.** _____ 2166

fort stood 103	Several boys climbed to the top of the tower. 104
slowly 291	a. a *very* high mountain b. drove *very* slowly Can the word *very* modify either an adjective or an adverb? (*Yes, No*) 292
b 479	There are a small number of special adverbs that modify other modifiers—both adjectives and adverbs. a. He took a *very* fast train. b. He talks *very* fast. In which sentence does the adverb *very* modify another adverb? ____ 480
lay 667	Terry's bicycle *lies* on the sidewalk. If you changed this sentence from present to past, you would need to change *lies* to _____. 668
a. interest b. visitors 855	Underline the word in each group with which the verb would need to agree: a. The reason for his good grades . . . b. My cousin with several friends . . . 856
shortest 1043	I chose the *smallest* of the five puppies. If we changed the number of puppies from **five** to **two**, we would change the adjective *smallest* to _____. 1044

Our neighbors and we 1231	The engineer took (*we, us*) fellows down to see the engine room. 1232
who 1418	all animals (*who, that*) 1419
back. A 1605	Its siren was screaming, he must get out of its way. _____ 1606
Yes 1792	A comma should generally be used when a sentence begins with (*the main statement, an introductory word group*). 1793
Bob's 1979	*Bob's* **locker is right next to** *ours.* We do not put an apostrophe in *ours* because it is a possessive (*noun, pronoun*). 1980
Empire State Building 2166	The employees of the Globe insurance company were entertained at the Oakland golf club. _____ 2167

boys climbed 104	**The car ahead of us suddenly stopped.** 105

Yes
 	
292
	You have just become acquainted with a special kind of adverb. This kind of adverb can modify either an adjective or an adverb.
	
	    a. **A** *very* **heavy snow fell.**
	    b. **The snow fell** *very* **fast.**
	
	The adverb *very* modifies an adverb in sentence (*a, b*).
	293

b 480	Many adjectives can be changed into adverbs. The adverb form of the adjective *brave* is _____. 481
lay 668	PRESENT SIMPLE PAST PAST WITH HELPER **lie** (in bed) **lay** **(have) lain** After *have, has,* or *had,* we use the word _____. 669
a. reason b. cousin 856	Should a verb ever be made to agree with the object of a preposition that follows the subject? (*Yes, No*) 857
smaller 1044	Adding –*er* or –*est* to long words would make them very clumsy to pronounce. Therefore, instead of saying *particularer*, we say *more particular*. Instead of saying *particularest*, we say *most particular*. The second degree of the adjective *wonderful* would be (*more wonderful, wonderfuller*). 1045

Lesson 42 Using the Right Pronouns in a Story

[Frames 1234-1256]

---

that

1419

our neighbor (*which, who*)

1420

---

screaming. He

1606

As he put on more speed, the fire engine increased its speed, too.

_____

1607

---

an introductory
word group

1793

If the introductory word group is short, the comma may be omitted.

a. *During the argument*, **a crowd had gathered.**
b. *During the argument between the two drivers*, **a crowd had gathered.**

From which sentence might you omit the comma? _____

1794

---

pronoun

1980

a. **Bobs** *locker* **is right next to** *our's.*
b. **Bob's** *locker* **is right next to** *ours.*
c. **Bob's** *locker* **is right next to** *our's.*

Which sentence is correct? _____

1981

Insurance
Company,
Golf Club

2167

A new theater will be built right across from the Ambassador hotel.

_____

2168

car stopped 105	**In the morning we start for California.** 106
b 293	We are now ready to write a full definition of an adverb: An adverb is a word that is used to modify a verb or another modifier. By "another modifier," we mean either an adjective or an _____. 294
bravely 481	a. **Frank** *was* **our guide.** b. **Frank** *hired* **an Indian guide.** One sentence contains an action verb; the other, a linking verb. Which sentence contains the linking verb? ____ 482
lain 669	Write the correct past form of **lie:** **The injured man must** *have* _____ **there for an hour.** 670
No 857	**One . . . is loose.** This sentence is correct. If you added the prepositional phrase *of my teeth*, would you need to make the verb plural? (*Yes, No*) 858
more wonderful 1045	The third degree of the adjective *interesting* would be (*interestingest, most interesting*). 1046

Each sentence in the following story presents a problem in the choice of pronouns. Underline the correct pronoun or pronouns in each sentence.

When my friend Pete and (*I, me*) were six years old, we were full of schemes for making money.

1234

---

who

1420

a large robin (*that, who*)

1421

Correct

1607

Soon he was doing nearly fifty, his truck could go no faster.

_____

1608

---

a

1794

a. *When we finally reached the station,* **the train had already left.**
b. *When we arrived,* **the train had already left.**

From which sentence might you omit the comma? ____

1795

---

b

1981

Add *one* apostrophe to this sentence:

We put *theirs* in *Tonys* car.

1982

Hotel

2168

The Fremont high school holds its graduation exercises in the Beverly theater.

_____

2169

<u>we</u> <u>start</u> 106	**The principal very often comes to our games.** 107
adverb 294	*very* **difficult**　　*so* **difficult**　　*terribly* **difficult** *rather* **difficult**　　*too* **difficult**　　*extremely* **difficult** *slightly* **difficult**　*quite* **difficult**　*somewhat* **difficult** We might say that all the italicized adverbs increase or decrease the "power" of the adjective _____. 295
a 482	a. **We** *looked* **in every corner.** b. **The restaurant** *looked* **clean.** In which sentence is *looked* used as a linking verb? ____ 483
lain 670	Write the correct past form of **lie:** 　**The old trunk** *had* _____ **in our attic for years.** 671
No 858	a. **One of my teeth** *is* **loose.** b. **One of my teeth** *are* **loose.** Which sentence is correct? ____ 859
most interesting 1046	With some adjectives and adverbs of two syllables, we can use either method: FIRST DEGREE　SECOND DEGREE　THIRD DEGREE 　　**happy**　　　　　**happi<u>er</u>**　　　　　**happi<u>est</u>** or:　**happy**　　　**<u>more</u> happy**　　　**<u>most</u> happy** Another two-syllable word that can be handled either way is (*regular, lovely, courteous*). 1047

I 1234	It was the day after Halloween, and the previous night (*we, us*) boys had covered the neighborhood very thoroughly, begging for treats. 1235
that 1421	Lesson **49** Putting Adjective Clauses to Work [Frames 1423-1447]
fifty. His 1608	Joe became very nervous, and he looked back again. _____ 1609
b 1795	In this and the following frames, put a comma after each introductory word group. If the main statement of the sentence comes first, make no change. **For the youngsters with ice skates the winter was a great disappointment.** 1796
Tony's 1982	**We put *theirs* in *Tony's* car.** We do not put an apostrophe in *theirs* because it is a possessive (*noun, pronoun*). 1983
High School, Theater 2169	**The Redeemer lutheran church uses the parking lot of the Jordan building.** _____ 2170

principal <u>comes</u> 107	**A young man in a raincoat jumped out of the car.** 108
difficult 295	*very* **neatly** *so* **neatly** *rather* **neatly** *quite* **neatly** *too* **neatly** *somewhat* **neatly** Here the italicized adverbs increase or decrease the "power" of the adverb _____. 296
b 483	Every linking verb must be completed by a (*direct object, subject complement*). 484
lain 671	Write the missing forms of **lie:** PRESENT SIMPLE PAST PAST WITH HELPER **lie** _____ (**have**) _____ 672
a 859	Remember that **doesn't** means **does not,** and **don't** means **do not.** Underline the verb that is always singular: **doesn't** **don't** 860
lovely 1047	a. **I have never had a** *happier* **day.** b. **I have never had a** *more happy* **day.** Are both sentences correct? (*Yes, No*) 1048

we 1235	Pete had collected as much as (*I*, *me*). 1236
	We often write a sentence that states a fact about a person or thing in the previous sentence. a. **We found a robin.** b. **It couldn't fly.** Sentence *b* states a fact about the noun _____ in sentence *a*. 1423
Correct 1609	His pursuer was still at his heels, the driver was waving his arms wildly. _____ 1610
skates, 1796	Stores often have sales at the end of the year. 1797

pronoun
 	
1983
	a. **We put** *their's* **in** *Tony's* **car.**
	    b. **We put** *theirs* **in** *Tonys* **car.**
	    c. **We put** *theirs* **in** *Tony's* **car.**
	
	Which sentence is correct? ____
	
	1984

Lutheran Church, Building 2170	The Bingham motor company donated an ambulance to our hospital. _____ 2171

man jumped 108	**The smoke from the factory spreads over the entire neighborhood.** 109

neatly
 	
296
	Because adverbs like *very, quite, rather,* and *extremely* control the power of other modifiers, we can think of them as "power" adverbs.
	
	     a. **a** *rather* **jealous person**
	     b. **an** *extremely* **jealous person**
	
	The adverb has more power in (*a, b*).
	
	297

subject complement 484	A subject complement always refers back to the _____ of the sentence. 485
lay, lain 672	Now let's look at the verb **lay,** with which **lie** is sometimes confused: **To lay** means "to put *something* down." **You can** *lay* **your coat on a chair.** What object do you *put down* in this sentence? _____ 673
doesn't 860	<u>One . . . doesn't open.</u> This sentence is correct. If you added the prepositional phrase *of these windows,* would you need to make the verb plural? (*Yes, No*) 861

Yes
 	
1048
	Form the second degree of a word by adding either –*er* or the word *more,* never both.
	
	     a. **Oleo is** *cheaper* **than butter.**
	     b. **Oleo is** *more cheaper* **than butter.**
	
	Which sentence is correct because there is no duplication? ____
	
	1049

I 1236	Our collection of candy, cookies, and fruit was too much for (*he, him*) **and** (*I, me*) **to eat.** 1237

robin
 	
1423
	See how we can combine two such sentences.
	
	    a. **We found a robin.** b. **It couldn't fly.**
	       We found a robin *that couldn't fly.*
	
	We combined these two sentences by changing sentence *b* to an adjective _____.
	
	1424

heels. The 1610	**He didn't dare stop now, the fire truck would crash into him.** _____ 1611
No comma 1797	**When children pick up magazines** **they usually read the advertisements first.** 1798

c
 	
1984
	a. *Judys* **house is closer than** *yours*.
	    b. *Petes* **dog was chasing the** *Neffs* **cat.**
	    c. *Ours* **has won more games than** *theirs*.
	
	Which sentence requires *no* apostrophes? ____
	
	1985

Motor Company 2171	**Can you think of a name for a stamp club we are starting at the Cooke school?** _____ 2172

smoke spreads	**The last leaves on the tree finally fluttered to the ground.**
109	110

b	a. **a** *terribly* **cold day** b. **a** *fairly* **cold day** The adverb has more power in (*a, b*).
297	298

subject	a. **Walter became a** *doctor*. b. **Walter called a** *doctor*. In which sentence is the noun *doctor* a subject complement because it refers back to the subject? ____
485	486

coat	**To lay** means "to put *something* down." Never use this word unless you mention the "something" that is *put down* or *moved* somewhere. **Don't** *lay* **the wet towel on the table.** Which object should you not *put down*? _____
673	674

No	a. **One of the windows** *don't* **open.** b. **One of the windows** *doesn't* **open.** Which sentence is correct? ____
861	862

a	WRONG: **Oleo is** *more cheaper* **than butter.** This sentence is wrong because the comparison is duplicated by the use of both *–er* and the adverb _____.
1049	1050

him, me

1237

"What can we do with all (*those, them*) things?" I asked Pete.

1238

---

clause

1424

Let's see how this is done:

    a. **I have a friend.**   b. **He plays the accordion.**

Sentence *b* states a fact about the noun _____ in sentence *a*.

1425

---

now. The

1611

This mad chase must end he would turn off at the next street.

_____

1612

---

magazines,

1798

We could hardly hear the announcement   because everybody was chattering.

1799

---

c

1985

---

    a. *Judys* **house is closer than** *yours.*
    b. *Petes* **dog was chasing the** *Neffs* **cat.**
    c. *Ours* **has won more games than** *theirs.*

Which sentence requires *two* apostrophes? ____

1986

School

2172

Lesson **76** **Capitals for Calendar Items and Brand Names**

[Frames 2174-2196]

leaves fluttered	When you analyze a sentence, always look for the (*subject, verb*) first.
110	111

a	**They served a slightly tough steak.**
	To *increase* the power of the adjective **tough,** you would
	change the adverb _____.
298	299

a	A subject complement can be a noun, a pronoun, or an adjective.
	a. **The driver was** *Carl.*
	b. **The driver was** *he.*
	c. **The driver was** *careful.*
	The subject complement is an adjective in sentence ____.
486	487

towel	After you *lay* something down, it *lies* there until it is moved somewhere else.
	You *lay* **your books down, and they** _____ **there.**
674	675

b	Underline the correct verb:
	One of the streets (*don't, doesn't*) **run through.**
862	863

more	Underline the correct choice:
	I have never seen a (*bluer, more bluer*) **sky.**
1050	1051

The problem of what to do with all our loot puzzled Pete as well as (*I, me*).

1239

---

friend

1425

a. **I have a friend.**   b. **He plays the accordion.**

Because sentence *b* states a fact about **friend** in sentence *a*, we can change it to an adjective clause.

The adjective clause will modify the noun _____ in sentence *a*.

1426

---

end. He

1612

Joe made the turn on two wheels, the tires screeched.

_____

1613

No comma

1799

Although the sun is 93 million miles away   it can burn a person's skin badly.

1800

---

b

1986

Remember that **its** is a possessive pronoun. Don't confuse it with **it's,** which is a shortened form of **it is.**

Underline the correct word:

Don't disturb (*its, it's*) nest.

1987

Capitalize the names of days of the week, months, and holidays.

Wednesday   February   Christmas

Copy and add capital letters to two words.

We will meet on the first tuesday in october.

2174

verb	When you change a sentence from present to past time, or from past to present time, the only word that changes is the _____.
111	112

slightly	**Howard drove frightfully fast.** To *decrease* the power of the adverb **fast,** you would change the adverb _____.
299	300

c	The verb **be** is the most common linking verb. FORMS OF *BE:* **is, am, _____—was, _____, been** Underline the two forms of **be** that are missing in the above line: **do are has will were**
487	488

lie	Here are the forms of the verb **lay:** PRESENT SIMPLE PAST PAST WITH HELPER **lay** (to put) **laid** **(have) laid** The simple past form and the helper form used with *have, has,* or *had* are (*alike, different*).
675	676

doesn't	In this and the following frames, find the subject of the sentence and underline it. Then underline the verb that agrees with the subject. Pay no attention to the prepositional phrase. **The demand for tickets** (*is, are*) **enormous.**
863	864

bluer	Form the third degree of a word by adding either *–est* or the word *most,* never both.
	
	      a. **Julie has the** *most latest* **records.**
	      b. **Julie has the** *latest* **records.**
	Which sentence is correct because there is no duplication? _____

1051	1052

me

1239

(*Pete he, He*) thought the matter over for a few seconds.

1240

---

friend

1426

Here is the sentence that we shall change to an adjective clause:

He plays the accordion.

Since our clause will modify the noun **friend,** we shall start our clause with the clause signal (*which, who*).

1427

---

wheels. The

1613

He was about to breathe a sigh of relief when he noticed the fire truck still behind him.

_____

1614

---

away,

1800

From the top of a skyscraper   the people and cars look like toys.

1801

---

its

1987

The possessive pronoun **its**—just like **yours, hers, ours,** and **theirs**—is written without an apostrophe.

Underline the correct word:

(*It's, Its*) **wing must be broken.**

1988

Tuesday, October

2174

There is more than one way of referring to some holidays.

Thanksgiving   Thanksgiving Day
New Year   New Year's   New Year's Day

When the word **day** is part of the name of a holiday, do we capitalize it? (*Yes, No*)

2175

verb 112	If the verb of a sentence is *disappeared*. find the subject by asking yourself, "_____ or _____ *disappeared?*" 113
frightfully 300	When we say that adverbs can modify other modifiers, we mean that they can modify _____ and _____. 301
are, were 488	FORMS OF *BE:* is, _____, are—_____, were, been Underline the two forms of **be** that are missing in the above line: **am** **did** **can** **was** **have** 489

alike
 	
676
	PRESENT SIMPLE PAST PAST WITH HELPER
	  pay **paid** **(have) paid**
	  lay **laid** **(have) laid**
	The verb **pay** is regular because both past forms end in *–d.*
	Is the verb **lay** regular, too? (*Yes, No*)
	
	677

demand, is 864	**Only one of my parents** (*were, was*) **at home.** 865
b 1052	WRONG: **Julie has the** *most latest* **records.** This sentence is wrong because the comparison is dupli- cated by the use of both *–est* and the adverb _____. 1053

He 1240	Then Pete said, "Why don't (*we, us*) guys sell (*them, those*) things back to our neighbors?" 1241
who 1427	We put the clause signal *who* in front of the sentence and omit any unnecessary words: *who* ~~He~~ plays the accordion. We end up with the clause _____. 1428
Correct 1614	He stopped his truck, there was nothing else to do. _____ 1615
skyscraper, 1801	You are safe from the lightning when you hear the sound of the thunder. 1802
Its 1988	An apostrophe should be used in every possessive (*noun, pronoun*). 1989
Yes 2175	Copy and add capital letters to four words that should be capitalized: I remembered that labor day is always the first monday in september. _____ 2176

Lesson 5 Verbs That Serve as Helpers

[Frames 115-146]

adjectives, adverbs

301

However, most adverbs modify verbs.

When?   Where?   How?   How much?   How often?

These are questions that we can ask about verbs.

Words that answer these questions are _____.

302

am, was

489

a. **cooked, sold, built, spoke, opened**
b. **was, seemed, became, appeared, looked**

Which group of verbs could be used as linking verbs? ____

490

Yes

677

We ... our work aside.
We *had* **... our work aside.**

In both sentences we would use the same form of the verb

lay. This form would be _____.

678

one, was

865

The sharp turns in this road (*makes, make*) **it dangerous.**

866

most

1053

In this and the following frames, underline the word or words that make the comparison correctly:

Which is (*more, most*) **interesting—the book or the movie?**

1054

we, those 1241	(*He, Him*) and (*I, me*) agreed to start with our neighbors, the Stokeses. 1242
who plays the accordion 1428	**I have a friend** *who plays the accordion.* We put the adjective clause right after the noun _____, which it modifies. 1429
truck. There 1615	**Two firemen jumped off and rushed with fire extinguishers to the back of his truck.** _____ 1616
No comma 1802	**Striking a piece of rough ice** **the hockey player rolled over several times.** 1803
noun 1989	POSSESSIVE PRONOUNS: **yours, hers, ours, theirs** Should these words ever be written with apostrophes? (*Yes, No*) 1990
Labor Day, Monday, September 2176	a. **Banks are closed on Washington's birthday.** b. **We are planning a party for Arlene's birthday.** In which sentence should **birthday** be capitalized because it is part of the name of a national holiday? ____ 2177

So far we have been working with one-word verbs, but with only single verbs, we often can't say what we mean.

Joe can go.   **Joe could go.**   **Joe must go.**

Joe will go.   **Joe should go.**   **Joe might go.**

Do these sentences have the same meaning? (*Yes. No*)

115

---

adverbs

302

One of these groups of adverbs can modify verbs; the other can modify other modifiers:

    a. **very, too, quite, rather, somewhat, extremely**
    b. **recently, truthfully, politely, stubbornly, promptly**

Which group can modify other modifiers? _____

303

---

b

490

We drove . ? . the park.

Any word that would fit into the blank space in this sentence would be a *pre* _____ .

491

---

laid

678

Now let's compare the forms of the verbs **lie** and **lay**:

PRESENT	SIMPLE PAST	PAST WITH HELPER
lie (in bed)	**lay**	**(have) lain**
lay (to put)	**laid**	**(have) laid**

One verb has three different forms, and the other has only two. Which verb has three different forms? _____

679

---

turns, make

866

The removal of the roots (*takes, take*) **considerable time.**

867

---

more

1054

Of the three brothers, Dave is the (*more, most*) **successful.**

1055

He, I 1242	Our families and (*they, them*) were very good friends. 1243
friend 1429	Here is another pair of sentences to combine: a. **Mother bought a dress.** b. **She didn't like the dress.** Suppose that we want to change sentence *b* to an adjective clause that will modify the noun **dress** in sentence *a*. Since this clause will modify the noun **dress**, we shall start our clause with the clause signal (*who, which*). 1430
Correct 1616	Now Joe understood everything, his truck was on fire. _____ 1617
ice, 1803	You will find the products of American factories in every country in the world. 1804
No 1990	In this and the following frames, underline the correct word in each italicized pair. (*Yours, Your's*) **is easier than** (*Helens, Helen's*) **recipe.** 1991

a
 	
2177
	Do *not* capitalize the names of the seasons.
	
	      spring winter
	      summer fall, autumn
	
	Fill each space with a small or capital letter, as the word requires:
	
	      Next ____uesday is the first day of ____inter.
	
	2178

These sentences have the same **main verb,** the word **go:**

Joe can go.	Joe could go.	Joe must go.
Joe will go.	Joe should go.	Joe might go.

No

Each time we change the verb before the *main verb* **go,**

the meaning of the sentence _____.

115

116

---

a

Underline two adverbs:

His older sister typewrites quite rapidly.

303

304

---

preposition

A preposition shows the *rel*_____ between
the noun or pronoun that follows it and some other word
in the sentence.

491

492

---

lie

PRESENT	SIMPLE PAST	PAST WITH HELPER
lie (in bed)	lay	(have) lain
lay (to put)	laid	(have) laid

Here is something that sometimes causes confusion:
The word **lay,** which means "to put *something* down," is

also the simple past form of the verb _____.

679

680

---

removal, takes

One of your lines (*don't, doesn't*) **rhyme well.**

867

868

---

most

We took the (*shorter, shortest*) **of the two routes.**

1055

1056

they	When Mr. Stokes saw (*we, us*) boys at the door with our Halloween baskets, he looked very surprised.
1243	1244
which	We put the clause signal *which* in front of the sentence and omit any unnecessary words. *which* **She didn't like ~~the dress~~.** We end up with the clause _____.
1430	1431
everything. His	**Lesson 56 Three Words That Cause Run-ons** [Frames 1619-1650]
1617	
No comma	Before Ann went into the water she felt it with her toes.
1804	1805
Yours, Helen's	(*Ken's, Kens*) radio gets more stations than (*theirs, their's*).
1991	1992
T, w	Fill in the missing letters: Our ____pring vacation comes in ____pril.
2178	2179

changes 116	**Joe can go.** **Joe could go.** **Joe must go.** **Joe will go.** **Joe should go.** **Joe might go.** A verb that helps the main verb to express our meaning more exactly is called a **helping verb**—or just a **helper**. The shortest helper in the above sentences is the word _____. 117
quite rapidly 304	Underline two adverbs: **A very strange accident occurred recently.** 305
relationship 492	After every preposition, we expect to find a noun or pro- noun that is called its _____. 493
lie 680	**He *lay* on the beach for an hour.** In this sentence, *lay* does not mean "to put something down." Instead, it is the simple past form of the verb _____. 681
One, doesn't 868	**Crowds from the football game (*jam, jams*) the streets.** 869
shorter 1056	**Which one of these three dresses do you think is the** (*prettier, prettiest*)? 1057

us 1244	"Are you fellows here again?" he asked Pete and (*I, me*). 1245

which she
didn't like
 	
1431
	After you change a sentence to an adjective clause, be sure to put the clause right after the word it modifies.
	
	    a. **A boy saw the accident.**
	    b. *who was standing on the corner.*
	
	The adjective clause *who was standing on the corner* should be put after the noun (*boy, accident*).
	
	1432

	A run-on sentence is a collision between two sentences. In this lesson, we shall look at some of the words that cause these collisions. **I approached the colt. The colt ran away.** Does each sentence have a subject and a verb? (*Yes, No*) 1619
water, 1805	**Although goats like to explore rubbish heaps** **they do not eat tin cans.** 1806
Ken's, theirs 1992	**My** (*sisters, sister's*) **violin was not in** (*its, it's*) **case.** 1993
s, A 2179	Fill in the missing letters: **Children look forward to ____alloween in the ____all.** 2180

can 117	Joe can go. Joe could go. Joe must go. Joe will go. Joe should go. Joe might go. The longest helper in the above sentences is the word _____. 118

very, recently
 	
305
	Underline two adverbs:
	
	    My dad always rises early.
	
	    306

object 493	A group of words that begins with a preposition and ends with its object is called a prepositional _____. 494
lie 681	PRESENT SIMPLE PAST PAST WITH HELPER **lie** (in bed) **lay** **(have) lain** **lay** (to put) **laid** **(have) laid** Would you ever use **laid** to mean "rested in a flat position"? (*Yes, No*) 682
Crowds, jam 869	**The correction of these mistakes** (*requires, require*) **a great deal of time.** 870
prettiest 1057	**Chess is** (*more difficult, difficulter*) **than checkers.** 1058

"You beggars did such a good job last night," Mr. Stokes went on, "that there's hardly anything left in the house for (*we, us*) folks to eat."

1246

---

a. **A boy** *who was standing on the corner* **saw the accident.**
b. **A boy saw the accident** *who was standing on the corner.*

Which sentence is correct? ____

1433

I approached the colt. The colt ran away.

Now let's substitute the pronoun **It** for the subject **colt.**

I approached the colt. It ran away.

Does the second sentence still have a subject and a verb? (*Yes, No*)

1620

Lesson **63** Commas in a Series

[Frames 1808-1836]

There was (*nobodys, nobody's*) **name after the "(***Your's,*** Yours***) truly."**

1994

Capitalize the names of particular brands of products.

Buick   Kleenex   Jello   Lux

We spray our roses with (*protex, Protex***).**

2181

should	HELPERS: shall, will must, might may, can should, would, could How many helping verbs end with the same four letters? _____
118	119
always, early	Underline two adverbs: **Very many people visit there.**
306	307

phrase	A prepositional phrase can do the job of either an adjective or an adverb.
	
	    a. **I sat** *near the stage.*
	    b. **A seat** *near the stage* **was vacant.**
	
	In which sentence is the phrase used as an adverb? ___

494	495

No	Use the word **laid** only when you mention the "something" that is put down somewhere.
	
	    a. **I caught cold because I . . . in a draft.**
	    b. **I . . . my** *money* **on the counter.**
	
	In which sentence would **laid** be correct? ___

682	683
correction, requires	**One of the ten-dollar bills** (*were, was*) **counterfeit.**
870	871
more difficult	**This is the** (*dangerousest, most dangerous*) **animal in the entire zoo.**
1058	1059

us 1246	"Jimmie and (*I, me*) aren't begging," explained Pete. "We just thought that maybe we could sell you something." 1247
a 1433	a. **She served custard to the child** *that was full of lumps.* b. **She served custard** *that was full of lumps* **to the child.** In which sentence is the clause placed correctly next to the word it modifies? ____ 1434
Yes 1620	It I approached the colt. ~~The colt~~ ran away. **It ran away** is a complete sentence. It is just as clear as **The colt ran away.** You know from the previous sentence that **It** refers to the _____. 1621
	A **series** is a number of similar things in a row. For example, we speak of a series of games or a series of parties when one comes after another. In baking a cake, selecting a recipe is the first in a <u>*s*_____</u> of several steps. 1808
nobody's, Yours 1994	(*Hers, Her's*) **was just as good as** (*our's, ours*). 1995
Protex 2181	**We feed our dog** (*Huskies, huskies*). 2182

three

119

HELPERS: **shall, will   must, might**
may, can   should, would, could

How many of these helping verbs begin with the letter **m**?

_____

120

Very, there

307

Underline two adverbs:

This paint dries extremely fast.

308

---

a

495

---

a. **We often played football** *in the vacant lot*.
b. **The boys** *in the vacant lot* **were playing football.**

In which sentence is the phrase used as an adjective? _____

496

---

b

683

The main point to remember is to use **lay**—never **laid**—as the simple past form of **lie** (in bed).

Underline the correct verb:

The boat (*lay, laid*) **on the beach all winter.**

684

One, was

871

Think about a sentence that has a *singular* subject followed by a prepositional phrase with a *plural* object. The verb in such a sentence should be (*singular, plural*).

872

---

most dangerous

1059

I have never read a (*more funnier, funnier*) **story.**

1060

I 1247	"Let me call Mrs. Stokes," he said. "She knows more about what we need than (*I, me*)." 1248
b 1434	**Every part is thoroughly tested** *that goes into a plane.* The italicized clause in this sentence is out of place. It should be put right after the noun _____, which it modifies. 1435

colt
 	
1621
	Be especially careful not to run two sentences together when the second sentence starts with **It**.
	
	    a. **I approached the colt, the colt ran away.**
	    b. **I approached the colt, it ran away.**
	
	Are both *a* and *b* run-on sentences? (*Yes, No*)
	
	1622

series 1808	Sentences often contain a *series* of words or word groups all doing the same job in the sentence. For example, a sentence might have a series of subjects, verbs, direct objects, subject complements, or modifiers. My *aunts, uncles,* **and** *cousins* **came to the party.** This sentence contains a series of (*subjects, objects*). 1809
Hers, ours 1995	**The** (*Watsons, Watsons'*) **car is newer than** (*theirs, their's*). 1996

Huskies
 	
2182
	Although brand names should be capitalized, the products that they identify should *not* be capitalized.
	
	   Krispie cornflakes **Walkaway shoes** **Vitex bread**
	
	    The program advertises Peerless (*tires, Tires*).
	
	2183

, three

The three verbs that follow are often used as helpers. Notice their various forms:

> **be (is, am, are — was, were, been)**
> **have (has, had)**
> **do (does, did)**

Which of these three verbs has the most forms? _____

120 · 121

---

extremely, fast

> **Frank is ...** *tall.*
> **Frank talks ...** *fast.*

To explain *how tall* Frank is or *how fast* he talks, we would need to use an (*adjective, adverb*).

308 · 309

---

b

Some words can be used as prepositions or adverbs.

> a. **The sun went** *down.*
> b. **We slid** *down* **the hill.**

In which sentence is *down* used as a preposition? ____

496 · 497

---

lay

The *-ing* forms of **lie** and **lay** are different:

> **lie** (in bed)—**lying**
> **lay** (to put)—**laying**

Underline the correct verb:

> **The dog was (***laying, lying***) near the hot stove.**

684 · 685

---

singular

Lesson **29** When the Verb Comes First

[Frames 874-902]

872

---

funnier

This was the (*longest, most longest***) trip I have ever taken.**

1060 · 1061

I 1248	When his wife came to the door, we showed Mr. Stokes and (*she, her*) all the goodies we had for sale. 1249
part 1435	**The house is nearly finished** *that the Hiltons are building.* The italicized clause in this sentence should be put after the noun _____, which it modifies. 1436
Yes 1622	a. **The plant was dry. It needed water.** b. **The plant was dry, it needed water.** Which arrangement is correct? _____ 1623
subjects 1809	**The cashier put the** *pennies, nickels,* **and** *dimes* **in separate piles.** This sentence contains a series of (*subjects, direct objects*). 1810
Watsons', theirs 1996	(*Its, It's*) **color is just like** (*our's, ours*). 1997
tires 2183	a. **The first prize was a Cookrite electric stove.** b. **The first prize was a Cookrite Electric Stove.** Which sentence is correctly capitalized? _____ 2184

be
 	
121
	be (is, am, are — was, were, been)
	
	Forms of **be** can serve either as main verbs or as helpers to other verbs. When **is** occurs as a helper, it is followed by the -*ing* form of the main verb.
	
	    a. **Tom is a painter.** b. **Tom is painting our house.**
	
	The verb **is** serves as a helper in sentence ____.
	
	           122

adverb 309	Besides modifying verbs, adverbs can also modify adjectives and other _____. 310
b 497	*Compound* means "having _____ or more parts." (How many?) 498

lying
 	
685
	Underline the correct verb:
	
	    The dishes were still (*lying, laying*) **on the table.**
	
	           686

	Two fish are in the bowl. The subject of this sentence is _____, and the verb is _____. 874
longest 1061	**Bob thought that a pound of nails would be** (*more heavier, heavier*) **than a pound of feathers.** 1062

her 1249	Mr. Stokes and (*she, her*) looked over our collection very carefully. 1250
house 1436	In this and the following frames, combine each pair of sentences by changing the italicized sentence to an adjective clause. Write the full sentence in the blank space. **We go to a park.** *It is near our house.* _____ _____ 1437
a 1623	Don't let other pronouns, either, lead you into writing run-on sentences. **Carol knew the answer. Carol raised her hand.** Suppose that we put **She** in place of **Carol** in the second sentence. Would it still be a separate sentence? (*Yes, No*) 1624

direct objects
 	
1810
	It takes at least *three* items to make a series.
	
	  a. **My** *aunts* **and** *uncles* **came to the party.**
	  b. **My** *aunts, uncles,* **and** *cousins* **came to the party.**
	
	Which sentence contains a series? ____
	1811

Its, ours 1997	Lesson **70** Contraction or Possessive Pronoun? [Frames 1999-2027]
a 2184	a. **The new station sells Road King Gasoline.** b. **The new station sells Road King gasoline.** Which sentence is correctly capitalized? ____ 2185

b 122	**have (has, had)** Forms of **have,** too, can serve either as main verbs or as helpers to other verbs. a. **I have found a job.** b. **I have a job.** The verb **have** serves as a helper in sentence ____. 123
adverbs 310	Adjectives can modify two kinds of words: *nouns* and *pronouns.* Adverbs can modify (*two, three*) kinds of words. 311
two 498	**We closed and locked all the windows.** This sentence has a compound (*verb, subject*). 499
lying 686	In this and the following frames, underline the correct forms of **lie** and **lay:** **Henry must (*lay, lie*) in bed for a few more days.** 687
fish, are 874	**Two fish are in the bowl.** As in most English sentences, the subject comes (*before, after*) the verb. 875
heavier 1062	Lesson **36** Avoiding the Double Negative Blunder [Frames 1064-1093]

she 1250	"(*Those, Them*) apples look very nice," Mrs. Stokes said. "I was just going to the store to buy some." 1251
We go to a park which (that) is near our house. 1437	Be sure to use **who** or **whom** to refer to persons, **which** to refer to things or animals, **that** to refer to any of these. **My brother made the touchdown.** *It won the game.* _____ _____ 1438
Yes 1624	a. **Carol knew the answer, she raised her hand.** b. **Carol knew the answer. She raised her hand.** Which arrangement is correct? _____ 1625
b 1811	**My** *aunts,* *uncles,* **and** *cousins* **came to the party.** This sentence has a series of three nouns used as subjects. How many commas are used to separate the nouns in this series? _____ 1812

	A few contractions and possessive pronouns sound just alike. Don't confuse them.
	
	    you're (*means* **you are**)
	    your (*means* **belonging to you**)
	
	Use **you're** only when you can put the two words _____
	
	_____ in its place.
	
	1999

b 2185	In this and the following frames, copy only the words to which capitals should be added, and write them with capitals. (Some of the uses of capitals studied in the two preceding lessons are included.) **Mother's day is always the second sunday in may.** _____ 2186

a 123	**do (does, did)** a. **I did my work.** b. **I did finish my work.** The verb **did** serves as a helper in sentence ___. 124
three 311	Adverbs can modify _____, _____, and other _____. 312
verb 499	**We locked all the doors and windows.** This sentence has a compound (*direct object, subject complement*). 500
lie 687	**Don't** (*lay, lie*) **the hot pan on the table.** 688
before 875	**Two <u>fish</u> <u>are</u> in the bowl.** We can express the same fact in another way: **There <u>are</u> two <u>fish</u> in the bowl.** Do both of these sentences have the same subject and verb? (*Yes, No*) 876
	A *negative* word says *no*. A *positive* word says *yes*. Underline two negative words: **some none ever never** *page 247* 1064

Those 1251	(*Mrs. Stokes she, She*) **got her purse and gave us fifteen cents.** 1252
My brother made the touchdown which (that) won the game. 1438	**A man came to our door.** *He was a salesman.* _____ _____ (Be sure to put the clause next to the noun it modifies.) 1439

b
 	
1625
	The word **then** is an adverb that tells *when*—just like **now, soon, yesterday,** or **recently. Then** is not a conjunction like **and.** It has no power to join sentences.
	
	    a. **We played tennis,** *then* **we went swimming.**
	    b. **We played tennis,** *and* **we went swimming.**
	
	Which is a run-on sentence? _____
	1626

two 1812	**My** *aunts, uncles,* **and** *cousins* **came to the party.** Notice that commas are used *between* the items of a series. Is there a comma before the first item in this series? (*Yes, No*) 1813
you are 1999	To show ownership, use the possessive pronoun (*you're, your*). 2000
Day, Sunday, May 2186	**I spent the summer on a small island in Georgian bay.** _____ 2187

There are several ways of showing present, past, and future time. To express some of them, we must use one or more helpers before the main verb.

PRESENT: a. **I talk.**   b. **I am talking.**

A helper is used with the main verb to show present time in (*a, b*).

125

---

verbs, adjectives, adverbs

312

Lesson **11** Linking Verbs and the Subject Complement

[Frames 314-349]

---

direct object

500

The connecting words **and, but,** and **or,** which are used to connect compound parts, are called *con*_____.

501

---

lay

688

Mother (*laid, lay*) **a cold cloth on my forehead.**

689

Yes

876

a. **Two** <u>fish</u> <u>are</u> **in the bowl.**

b. **There** <u>are</u> **two** <u>fish</u> **in the bowl.**

In which sentence does the verb come *before* the subject?

____

877

---

none, never

1064

a. **Somebody was at the door.**

b. **Nobody was at the door.**

Which sentence is negative? ____

1065

She 1252	(*I and my friend, My friend and I*) **were delighted with our quick success in making a sale.** 1253
A man who (that) was a salesman came to our door. 1439	**The Bergs have a dog.** *It chases cars.* _____ _____ 1440
a 1626	a. **I put down the right answer,** *then* **I changed it.** b. **I put down the right answer.** *Then* **I changed it.** **Which arrangement is correct? ____** 1627
No 1813	**My** *aunts, uncles,* **and** *cousins* **came to the party.** Is there a comma after the last item in this series? (*Yes, No*) 1814
your 2000	a. **I think ... right.** b. **You missed ... bus.** In which sentence would the words **you are** make sense? ____ 2001
Bay 2187	**On saturday afternoon, the Atlas theater will give away a victor bicycle.** _____ 2188

PAST: **I talked.   I have talked.   I had talked.**
I have been talking.   I had been talking.

In these sentences that show past time, some of the main verbs have as many as (*one, two, three*) helpers.

b

125

126

Earl   chairman

Do these two nouns by themselves form a sentence? (*Yes, No*)

314

---

conjunctions

When you connect two separate sentences with the conjunction **and, but,** or **or,** you make a _____ sentence.

501

502

---

laid

Dad (*laid, lay*) **back in his chair and fell asleep.**

689

690

---

b

We start many sentences with the words **There is** and **There are** or **There was** and **There were.** In all such sentences, the verb comes ahead of the subject.

Underline the subject with one line and the verb with two lines:

There are some good stories in this book.

877

878

---

b

Underline the word that makes this sentence negative:

Nobody was at the door.

1065

1066

My friend and I 1253	**Mr. and Mrs. Stokes seemed just as pleased as** (*we, us*) **with the transaction.** 1254
The Bergs have a dog which (that) chases cars. 1440	**I have a friend.** *His father owns a speedboat.* (Try *whose.*) _____ _____ 1441

b
 	
1627
	A new sentence can begin with **Then**—just as it can begin with any other word that tells *when*.
	
	    The sky darkened. *Soon* **it began to rain.**
	    The sky darkened. *Later* **it began to rain.**
	    The sky darkened. *Then* **it began to rain.**
	
	Is each pair of sentences correct? (*Yes, No*)
	1628

No
 	
1814
	Put commas *between* the items in a series—not before or after the series.
	
	    a. **We put the,** *pennies, nickels,* **and** *dimes* **in piles.**
	    b. **We put the** *pennies, nickels,* **and** *dimes,* **in piles.**
	    c. **We put the** *pennies, nickels,* **and** *dimes* **in piles.**
	
	Which sentence is punctuated correctly? ____
	1815

a 2001	a. **I think ... right.** b. **You missed ... bus.** In which sentence would the contraction **you're** be correct? ____ 2002
Saturday, Theater, Victor 2188	**St. Agnes church was very crowded on good friday.** _____ 2189

FUTURE: **I shall walk.   I shall be walking.
I shall have walked.**

Is the main verb used without a helper in any one of these sentences that show future time? (*Yes, No*)

127

Earl . . . chairman.

Underline the one word that you could add to turn the above words into a sentence:

good   is   new

315

---

a. **The little colt came to the fence and licked my hand.**
b. **The little colt came to the fence and I patted its head.**

In which sentence should a comma be inserted before the conjunction **and?** ____

Note to student:
You are now ready for Unit Test 2.

503

We (*laid, lay*) **on the beach and watched the water-skiers.**

691

We often start sentences, too, with the words **Here is** and **Here are**. In these sentences the verbs also come before the subjects.

Here is your pen.

Underline the subject and the verb:

Here are your sandwiches.

879

Here is a list of negative words:

**not (n't)   never   no one   nothing
none   neither   nobody   nowhere**

Every one of these negative words, just like the word **no,**

begins with the letter ____.

1067

we 1254	We thanked Mr. Stokes and (*she, her*) and went on our way. 1255
I have a friend whose father owns a speedboat. 1441	The heat wave is the worst one in ten years. *It started last week.* _____ _____ 1442
Yes 1628	a. **The car slowed down. It stopped.** b. **The car slowed down.** *Then* **it stopped.** Is each pair of sentences correct? (*Yes, No*) 1629
c 1815	We can also have a series of verbs or modifiers in a sentence. a. **Africa's** *dark, moist,* **and** *tangled* **forests are full of animal life.** b. **Jerry** *dressed,* **ate his breakfast, and** *hurried* **to school.** Which sentence contains a series of verbs? ____ 1816
a 2002	Underline the correct word: **You missed (*you're, your*) bus.** 2003
Church, Good Friday 2189	**Have you seen the christmas display at the Whitman library?** _____ 2190

No 127	See what usually happens when we change a sentence from a statement to a question: STATEMENT: **Ellen can swim.** QUESTION: **Can Ellen swim?** The subject comes between the verb and its helper in the (*statement, question*). 128
is 315	**Earl is chairman.** We have now turned these words into a sentence by adding the verb _____. 316
b 503	UNIT 3: **GETTING YOUR VERB FORMS RIGHT** Lesson **17** See, *Do*, and **Go** [Frames 505-538]
lay 691	**Mother forgot where she had** (*laid, lain*) **her glasses.** 692
<u>are sandwiches</u> 879	In most of our sentences, we state the subject first. Then we select a _____ that agrees with it in number. 880
n 1067	a. **none** **never** **nobody** **nowhere** **nothing** b. **some** **ever** **somebody** **somewhere** **something** Which list of words is negative? ____ 1068

her 1255	Do you wonder that the neighbors predicted successful business careers for Pete and (*I, me*)? 1256
The heat wave which (that) started last week is the worst one in ten years. 1442	We took a narrow road. *It had many turns.* _____ _____ 1443
Yes 1629	Rita decided to make fudge._∧ She changed her mind. If we added the adverb **Then** at the point marked by the caret (∧), would we still have two separate sentences? (*Yes, No*) 1630
b 1816	To be a series, there must be at least (*two, three*) items. 1817

your
 	
2003
	Here are two more words that should not be confused:
	
	    they're (means **they are**)
	    their (means **belonging to them**)
	
	Use **they're** only when you can put the two words _____ _____ in its place.
	
	2004

Christmas, Library 2190	The Rex hardware company is giving away free samples of glasscote enamel this week. _____ 2191

question	128

a. **Ross lives on a farm.**
b. **Does Ross live on a farm?**

In which sentence does the subject come between the

verb and its helper—*a* or *b*? _____

129

---

is

316

To link means "to connect." We might, for example, link two chains together.

<u>Earl</u> **is chairman.**

In this little sentence, the verb **is** links the noun **chairman**

to the subject _____.

317

Most verbs show by their endings whether they mean present or past time.

    a. I *walk* **to school every day.**
    b. I *walked* **to school every day.**

In which sentence does the verb show past time? _____

505

---

laid

692

The dog must have (*laid, lain*) **down in a mud puddle.**

693

---

verb

880

However, in sentences that begin with words like **There is** and **Here are,** the verb comes first. Therefore, before selecting your verb, you must look ahead to see whether a

_____ or _____ subject is coming.

881

---

a

1068

Any verb that ends in **n't** is negative because **n't** means

_____.

1069

Lesson 43 Unit Review

We took a narrow road which (that) had many turns.

1443

We parked next to a fireplug. *Nobody had noticed it.*

_____

_____

1444

Yes

1630

The word **therefore** also causes many run-on sentences. **Therefore** is an adverb that tells *why*. It is not a conjunction like **and**. It has no power to join sentences.

    a. **My line broke,** *and* **the fish got away.**
    b. **My line broke,** *therefore* **the fish got away.**

Which is a run-on sentence? _____

1631

---

three

1817

a. **The men talked, and joked together for two hours.**
b. **The men talked, joked, and laughed together for two hours.**

One sentence does not contain a series of three items. From which sentence should the comma or commas be dropped? _____

1818

---

they are

2004

    a. **. . . car broke down.**
    b. **. . . coming over later.**

In which sentence would the two words **They are** make sense? _____

2005

Hardware Company, Glasscote

2191

We celebrate thanksgiving on the fourth thursday in november.

_____

2192

b 129	In the following question, underline the subject with one line, the main verb and its helper with two lines: **Must you study tonight?** 130
Earl 317	**Earl is chairman.** Any verb that links a word that follows it to the subject of the sentence is called a **linking verb**. Underline the linking verb: **The man was a detective.** 318
b 505	PRESENT: I *walk* PAST: I *walked* To change the verb *walk* from present to past, we merely add the letters _____. 506
lain 693	**Mother had** (*laid, lain*) **away all the gifts until Christmas.** 694
singular, plural 881	**There (was, were) only three boys in the class.** The subject that follows the verb in this sentence is the noun _____. 882
not 1069	a. **does** **could** **have** **was** **did** b. **doesn't** **couldn't** **haven't** **wasn't** **didn't** Which list of verbs is negative? _____ 1070

a. I, he, she, we, they
b. me, him, her, us, them

Which group of words would you use for the subjects of sentences? ____

1258

We parked next to a fireplug which (that) nobody had noticed.

1444

Friends gave us advice. *They had been to Mexico.*

_____

_____

1445

---

b

1631

a. I had read the book. *Therefore* I wanted to see the movie.
b. I had read the book, *therefore* I wanted to see the movie.

Which arrangement is correct? ____

1632

---

a

1818

a. **We were surrounded by a mountain of bundles, bags, and valises.**
b. **We were surrounded by a mountain of bundles, and bags.**

From which sentence should the comma or commas be dropped? ____

1819

---

b

2005

a. **... car broke down.**
b. **... coming over later.**

In which sentence would the contraction **They're** be correct? ____

2006

Thanksgiving, Thursday, November

2192

I plan to enter Norris high school in the fall.

_____

2193

<u>Must</u> <u>you</u> <u>study</u> tonight? 130	In this question, underline the subject with one line, the main verb and its helper with two lines: **Can this parrot talk?** 131
was 318	**The man was a detective.** The linking verb **was** shows that the **detective** and the **man** are (*the same, different*) person(s). 319
–ed 506	Underline the two verbs that show past time: **appear laughed open smiled** 507
laid 694	**My wallet was still (*lying, laying*) on the sidewalk.** 695
boys 882	**There (was, were) only three boys in the class.** Because the subject of this sentence is the plural noun **boys**, we would choose the plural verb _____. 883
b 1070	It takes only one negative word to make a sentence negative. **These roses don't have thorns.** The word that makes this sentence negative is _____. 1071

When a pronoun follows the word **than** or **as**, don't select your pronoun until you think of the missing word or words.

a. **The problem puzzled Jack more than** (*it puzzled*) *me*.
b. **Jack understood the problem no better than** *me* (*did*).

In which sentence is the object form *me* correct? ____

Friends who (that) had been to Mexico gave us advice.

The speaker told a story. *We thought it was very funny.*

_____

_____

The ice had melted. ∧ **We couldn't skate.**

If we added the adverb **Therefore** at the point marked by the caret (∧), would we still have two separate sentences? (*Yes, No*)

We generally use the conjunction **and** or **or** to connect the last two items in a series.

Our team practices on Monday, Wednesday, and Friday of each week.

The last two items in this series are connected by the conjunction _____.

Underline the correct word:

(*Their, They're*) **car broke down.**

Several stores on Drummond avenue sell mohawk sweaters.

_____

<u>Can this parrot</u> <u>talk?</u> 131	Before doing the next frames, take another look at these helping verbs, which have no other forms:
	
	    shall, will must, might
	    may, can should, would, could
	
	How many of these helpers have exactly five letters? _____
	<div align="right">132</div>

the same 319	**The building was a hospital.** The noun **hospital** refers to the same thing as the subject _____. <div align="right">320</div>
laughed, smiled 507	PRESENT: **chase wave smile taste** PAST: **chased waved smiled tasted** The present forms of these verbs already end in *e*. To change these verbs to the past, we do not need to add *–ed* but only _____. <div align="right">508</div>
lying 695	Lesson **23** *Sit and Set; Rise and Raise* <div align="right">[Frames 697-725]</div>
were 883	a. **There ... a big tree in our yard.** b. **There ... several big trees in our yard.** In which sentence would it be wrong to use the singular verb **is?** ____ <div align="right">884</div>
don't 1071	**These roses have no thorns.** The word that makes this sentence negative is _____. <div align="right">1072</div>

a 1259	When you use pronouns in pairs, use the same pronouns that you would if you used them one at a time. *He* **repaired the bike.** *I* **repaired the bike.** Now let's put these two sentences together: _____ and ____ repaired the bike. 1260
The speaker told a story which (that) we thought was very funny. 1446	**The crowd cheered Tony.** *His hit won the game.* (Try *whose*.) _____ _____ 1447
Yes 1633	Can the pronoun **it** or the adverb **then** or **therefore** start a new sentence? (*Yes, No*) 1634
and 1820	**Do not leave money, jewelry, or other valuables in your desk.** The last two items in this series are connected by the conjunction _____. 1821
Their 2007	Here are two more words to straighten out in your mind: **who's** (means **who is** *or* **who has**) **whose** (means **belonging to whom**) Do not use the contraction **who's** unless you can fit in the two words _____ or the two words _____. 2008
Avenue, Mohawk 2194	**We got our new ford right after easter and drove to the Smoky mountains.** _____ 2195

page 264

four 132	Here, once again, are the three verbs that can be used as either helpers or as main verbs: **be (is, am, are — was, were, been)** **have (has, had) do (does, did)** The verbs **was** and **been** are forms of the verb _____. 133
building 320	<u>Earl <u>is</u> .?..</u> This sentence must be completed. Any word that completes it might be called a _completer_. The grammar name for _completer_ is **complement**. The first _____ letters of the words _completer_ and _complement_ are the same. (How many?) 321
–d 508	a. **We** _washed_ **the car.** b. **We** _have washed_ **the car.** Both these sentences show past time. In which sentence does the verb consist of two words? ____ 509
	To sit means "to take a sitting position" or "to be in place." We say, "Don _sits_ in the front row" and "The dictionaries _sit_ on the top shelf." Supply the missing verb: **The patients _____ and wait for the doctor.** 697
b 884	a. **There ... several telephones in the office.** b. **There ... a telephone in the office.** Which sentence requires the plural verb **are**? ____ 885
no 1072	**These roses don't have thorns.** **These roses have no thorns.** How many negative words does each of these sentences have? _____ 1073

He, I	When you use a pronoun with a noun, use the same pronoun that you would if you used the pronoun alone.
	Del waited for *Bob*. **Del waited for** *me*.
	Del waited for Bob and _____.
1260	1261

The crowd cheered Tony, whose hit won the game.	Lesson **50** Using *–ing* Word Groups
1447	[Frames 1449-1471]

Yes	The words **it, then,** and **therefore** do not always start new sentences. They can come, too, in the middle of sentences.
	If you tease the dog, *it* **might bite you.**
	If you can't be a good loser, *then* **you had better not play.**
	New drivers, *therefore,* **should drive slowly.**
	Are these run-on sentences? (*Yes, No*)
1634	1635

or	When all the items in a series are connected by the conjunction **and** or **or,** do not use any commas at all.
	a. **The leaves turn** *red* **and** *brown* **and** *yellow* **in the autumn.**
	b. **The leaves turn** *red* *brown* **and** *yellow* **in the autumn.**
	Which sentence does *not* require any commas? _____
1821	1822

who is who has	**. . . paper did you correct?**
	Would the words **Who is** (or the words **Who has**) make sense in this sentence? (*Yes, No*)
2008	2009

Ford, Easter, Mountains	**The Belleville voters' club will hold its september meeting in our school auditorium.**
2195	2196

be 133	In this and the following frames, the main verb is printed in italics, and the first letter of one or more helping verbs is given. Complete the spelling of each helping verb. I *w*_____ *watching* **the steam shovel.** 134
six 321	**Earl is** *chairman.* Here the *complement* is the noun _____. The complement **chairman** refers to the same person as the subject _____. 322
b 509	**We** *have washed* **the car.** In this sentence the main verb *washed* is used with the helping verb _____. 510
sit 697	PRESENT SIMPLE PAST PAST WITH HELPER **sit** (on a chair) **sat** **(have) sat** Is the word **set** either one of the past forms of the verb **sit**? (*Yes, No*) 698
a 885	Underline the verb that agrees with the subject: **Here** (*is, are*) **the tickets to the game.** 886
one 1073	Using two negative words to make a single negative statement is a bad mistake in English. This mistake is called a **double negative.** WRONG: **These roses** *don't* **have** *no* **thorns.** To correct this sentence, you would need to omit either the word _____ or _____. 1074

In this and the following frames, underline the correct word or words in each sentence:

(*He, Him*) **and** (*I, me*) **learned this duet last summer.**

1262

Eileen has several hobbies. *They keep her busy.*
Eileen has several hobbies *that keep her busy.*

We combined these two sentences by changing the italicized sentence to an _____ clause.

1449

No

Do not capitalize **it, then,** or **therefore** unless the word group it follows is a complete sentence.

    a. **When I petted the cat,** *it* **scratched me.**
    b. **I petted the cat,** *it* **scratched me.**

Put a period after **cat,** and write *it* with a capital letter in (*a, b*).

1635

1636

---

a

The leaves turn *red* **and** *brown* **and** *yellow* **in the autumn.**

This sentence requires no commas because all the items

in the series are connected by the conjunction _____.

1822

1823

No

Underline the correct word:

(*Who's, Whose*) **paper did you correct?**

2009

2010

Voters' Club,
September

2196

Lesson **77** **Capitals for Titles and Names**

was 134	The key s _____ *fit* this lock. 135
chairman Earl 322	Because the complement we are studying refers back to the subject, it is called a **subject complement**. **These books are dictionaries.** The noun **books** is the subject, but the noun **dictionaries** is the *subject* _____. 323
have 510	**Bob** *has washed* **the car.** In this sentence the main verb *washed* is used with the helping verb _____. 511
No 698	PRESENT SIMPLE PAST PAST WITH HELPER **sit** (on a chair) **sat** **(have) sat** The simple past form and the helper form used with **have, has,** and **had** are (*alike, different*). 699
are 886	**There's** means **There is,** and **Here's** means **Here is.** The words **There's** and **Here's** should be used only before (*plural, singular*) subjects. 887
don't, no 1074	When you switch off a light, the light goes out. There is no use in pressing the switch again. In the same way, when you use one negative word, your sentence becomes negative, and adding a second negative word is useless. WRONG: **I didn't eat no breakfast this morning.** The two negative words are _____ and ___. 1075

He, I 1262	Have I ever told you what nearly happened to (*she, her*) and (*I, me*)? 1263

adjective
 	
 1449
	In this lesson we will learn how to combine sentences by using another device, the *–ing* word group.
	
	     a. **Jack walked down the aisle.**
	     b. *He looked for his friends.*
	
	 Sentence *b* states a fact about (*Jack, aisle*) in sentence *a*.
	 1450

b 1636	a. **Jan wore the dress,** *then* **she tried to return it.** b. **If Jan wears the dress,** *then* **she can't return it.** Only one of these is a run-on sentence. Put a period after **dress,** and write *then* with a capital letter in (*a, b*). 1637
and 1823	a. **We cannot** *see,* *smell,* **or** *taste* **pure air.** b. **We cannot** *see,* **or** *smell,* **or** *taste* **pure air.** From which sentence should the commas be dropped? ___ 1824
Whose 2010	**... the girl in the front seat?** Would the words **Who is** make sense in this sentence? (*Yes, No*) 2011
   	A word that shows a person's profession, rank, or office is called a **title.** **doctor** **professor** **captain** **mayor** **judge** These nouns can be used as _____. 2198

should 135	It *h* _____ *b* _____ *raining* **all day.** 136
complement 323	**These books are dictionaries.** The *subject* of a sentence usually comes before the verb. The *subject complement* usually comes _____ the verb. 324
has 511	**Someone** *had washed* **the car.** In this sentence the main verb *washed* is used with the helping verb _____. 512
alike 699	a. **We . . . in the balcony.** b. **We** *had* **. . . in the library.** In both sentences we would use the same form of the verb **sit.** This form would be _____. 700
singular 887	a. **Here are some biscuits for the dog.** b. **Here's some biscuits for the dog.** Which sentence is correct? ____ 888
didn't, no 1075	a. **I ate no breakfast this morning.** b. **I didn't eat breakfast this morning.** c. **I didn't eat no breakfast this morning.** Which sentence is wrong because it contains a double negative? ____ 1076

her, me 1263	The Matsons and (*they, them*) promised to buy tickets from me. 1264
Jack 1450	a. **Jack walked down the aisle.** b. *He looked for his friends.* **Jack walked down the aisle,** *looking for his friends.* We changed sentence *b* to a word group that begins with a word that ends in *–ing*. This word is _____. 1451
a 1637	a. **Some of the people,** *therefore,* **had to stand.** b. **There weren't enough seats for all the people,** *therefore* **some of them had to stand.** Only one of these is a run-on sentence. Put a period after **people,** and write *therefore* with a capital letter in (*a, b*). 1638
b 1824	**We cannot** *see* **or** *smell* **or** *taste* **pure air.** This sentence requires no commas because all the items in the series are connected by _____. 1825
Yes 2011	Underline the correct word: (*Who's, Whose*) **the girl in the front seat?** 2012

titles
 	
2198
	Capitalize titles when they are used with personal names; for example, **Professor Dow, Captain Marsh, Judge Ross.**
	    a. **The boys admired their** *coach.*
	    b. **The boys admired** *coach* **Brady.**
	In which sentence should *coach* be capitalized because it is part of a person's name? ____
	
	2199

has (had) been 136	**Ralph** *m* _____ *h* _____ *taken* **the wrong road.** 137

after
 	
324
	Adjectives, as well as nouns, can be used as subject complements.
	
	     a. **Earl is** *chairman.*
	     b. **Earl is** *capable.*
	
	In which sentence is the subject complement not a noun, but an adjective? _____
	
	325

had 512	Most verbs show past time in these two ways: 1. By the simple past form that ends in *-ed*. 2. By the same simple past form combined with *have*, *has*, or *had*, which are called _____ *ing* verbs. 513
sat 700	The verb **sit** must not be confused with the verb **set**. **To set** means "to put or to place *something*." **We** *set* **the chairs around the desk.** What objects are put or placed somewhere in this sentence? _____ 701
a 888	a. **There's the names of our members.** b. **There are the names of our members.** Which sentence is correct? _____ 889
c 1076	a. **Chuck couldn't get along with anybody.** b. **Chuck couldn't get along with nobody.** Which sentence is wrong because it contains a double negative? _____ 1077

they 1264	Mr. Krantz appointed (*he, him*) and (*I, me*) as class representatives. 1265
looking 1451	*looking for his friends* We call this an –*ing* word group. It begins with the word *looking*, which ends with the three letters _____. 1452
b 1638	In this and in each of the following frames, you will find a sentence. If the sentence is correct, write *Correct* on the blank line. If the sentence is a run-on sentence, correct it like this: EXAMPLE: **We rang the bell, then we knocked on the door.** *bell. Then*　　　　(*Turn to the next frame.*) 1639
or (*or* conjunctions) 1825	In this and the following frames, add commas wherever the sentence contains a series. If a sentence does not contain a series, make no change. Remember that it takes *three* items to make a series. **Only Alaska Texas and California are larger than Montana.** 1826
Who's 2012	**It's** and **its** are the two words most often confused. 　　　　**it's** (means **it is** *or* **it has**) 　　　　**its** (means **belonging to it**) In the contraction **it's**, the apostrophe stands for the missing letter ____ or for the missing letters _____. 2013
b 2199	a. **A meeting was called by** *mayor* **Hurley.** b. **Our town will soon elect a new** *mayor.* In which sentence should *mayor* be capitalized because it is part of a person's name? ____ 2200

must (might, may) have	Pete *w* _____ *read* **the book as soon as he** *c* _____ *get* **it.**

---

b	**Earl is** *capable.* The adjective *capable* modifies the subject of the sentence, which is _____.

325

326

---

helping	**I ...** *locked* **the door.** If you added the helper *have* to the verb in this sentence, would you need to change the verb *locked*? (*Yes, No*)

513

514

---

chairs	After you **set** something down, it **sits** there until you move it somewhere else. We **set** the dog's dinner on the floor, and it _____ there until he eats it.

701

702

---

b	When we change **There is** or **There are** to **Is there** or **Are there,** the sentence becomes a question. In such a question, the verb still comes before the subject. **Are there any nuts in this ice cream?** The verb **Are** agrees with the plural subject _____.

889

890

---

b	Underline the correct word: **My dad never eats** (*no, any*) **onions.**

1077

1078

him, me 1265	**The Kings and** (*we, us*) **shop at the same market.** 1266
–ing 1452	Compare an *–ing* word group with a clause. CLAUSE: *who was looking for his friends* *–ING* WORD GROUP: *looking for his friends* Does an *–ing* word group, like a clause, have a subject and a verb? (*Yes, No*) 1453
	An empty bottle is not really empty, it is actually filled with air. —————————————————— 1640
Alaska, Texas, 1826	**Cleaners are not responsible for ornaments belts or buckles that are not removed from suits and dresses.** 1827
i ha 2013	Don't use **it's** unless the two words **it is** or the two words **it has** would fit in. a. ... **a rainy day.** b. ... **meal is ready.** In which sentence would **It is** make sense? ____ 2014
a 2200	**The** *lieutenant* **was praised by** *major* **Lozano.** The word that should be capitalized is (*lieutenant, major*). 2201

will, can	Yes, I d_____ *turn* off the alarm this morning.
138	139

Earl	a. **This book is** *heavy.* b. **This book is** *a dictionary.* In which sentence is the subject complement an adjective? ____
326	327

No	**Roy** *has corrected* **his test.** If you dropped the helper *has* in the above sentence, would you need to change the verb *corrected*? (Yes, No)
514	515

sits	Here are the forms of the verb **set:** PRESENT SIMPLE PAST PAST WITH HELPER **set** (to put) **set** **(have) set** This verb is different from all the other verbs we have studied because it has only _____ form. (How many?)
702	703

nuts	a. **Is there a seat for me?** b. **Are there a seat for me?** Which sentence is correct? ____
890	891

any	Most negative words begin with *n.* However, here are two negative words that do not begin with *n:* **hardly, scarcely.** **I could hardly see the sign.** The word that makes this sentence negative is _____.
1078	1079

we 1266	We couldn't find the Regans or (*they, them*) anywhere in the park. 1267
No 1453	Let's see how we change a sentence to an –*ing* word group: **He <u>looked</u> for his friends.** ↓ *looking* for his friends We drop the subject of the sentence, **He**. Then we change the verb **looked** to _____. 1454
empty. It 1640	**After you play this game a few times, you tire of it.** _____ 1641
ornaments, belts, 1827	**One should always keep a pad and pencil near the telephone.** 1828
a 2014	Underline the correct word: (*It's, Its*) a rainy day. 2015
Major 2201	**People were pleased that** *superintendent* **Baird promoted the brave** *officer*. The word that should be capitalized is (*superintendent, officer*). 2202

did 139	Underline the complete verb in each sentence. Remember that the complete verb includes all helpers that may be present. **Perry could eat an entire pie.** 140
a 327	A linking verb is usually followed by a subject complement. The most common linking verb is **be.** Memorize its various forms for the frames that follow: **FORMS OF** *BE:* **is, am, are—was, were, been** After each of the above verbs we may expect to find a _____ *complement.* 328
No 515	**Mother . . . all day.** **Mother** *has* **. . . all day.** Would the verb *cooked* be correct in both the above sentences? (*Yes, No*) 516
one 703	PRESENT: I . . . the table for breakfast every morning. SIMPLE PAST: I . . . the table for dinner last night. PAST WITH HELPER: I *have* . . . the table for three. Would the verb **set** be correct in all three of these sentences? (*Yes, No*) 704
a 891	a. **Is there any stamps in that drawer?** b. **Are there any stamps in that drawer?** Which sentence is correct? ____ 892
hardly 1079	a. **I could hardly see the sign.** b. **I couldn't hardly see the sign.** Which sentence is wrong because it contains a double negative? ____ 1080

them 1267	Nancy or (*she, her*) will serve as secretary. 1268
looking 1454	Jack walked down the aisle, *looking for his friends.* The *–ing* word group *looking for his friends* modifies the noun (*Jack, aisle*). 1455
Correct 1641	I got my haircut, then I discovered that I had left my money at home. ―――――――――――― 1642
No commas 1828	The high winds damaged houses barns trees and power lines throughout the state. 1829
It's 2015	. . . meal is ready. In this sentence, would the two words **It is** (or the two words **It has**) make sense? (*Yes, No*) 2016

Superintendent
 	
2202
	Also capitalize words that show family relationship when they are used *with* personal names; for example, **Uncle Don, Grandmother Harris.**
	
	    a. **I received a gift from my** *aunt.*
	    b. **I received a gift from my** *aunt* **Betty.**
	
	In which sentence should *aunt* be capitalized? ＿＿＿ 2203
	page 280

could eat 140	**Have you heard the news?** 141
subject 328	Fill in the two missing forms of the linking verb *be:* **FORMS OF** *BE:* **is, am, _____—was, were, _____.** 329

Yes
 	
516
	Verbs like **walk, lock, close,** and **save** are called **regular verbs** because we form their past by adding *–d* or *–ed*.
	
	    a. **play—played**
	    b. **write—wrote**
	    c. **march—marched**
	
	Which one of the above verbs is not regular? _____
	
	517

Yes 704	Let's compare this pair of similar verbs: PRESENT SIMPLE PAST PAST WITH HELPER **sit** (on a chair) **sat** **(have) sat** **set** (to put) **set** **(have) set** Would you ever use **set** to mean "to take a sitting position" or "to be in place"? (*Yes, No*) 705
b 892	In question sentences that begin with **Where** or **How much,** the verb also comes ahead of the subject. Underline the subject with one line and the verb with two lines: **Where** (*was, were*) **the keys?** 893
b 1080	**We scarcely had time to eat.** The word that makes this sentence negative is _____. 1081

she

1268

There was no room for the Linds and (*we, us*) in their car.

1269

Jack

1455

Jack walked down the aisle, *looking for his friends.*

This is a good sentence.

Must an *–ing* word group be next to the word it modifies? (*Yes, No*)

1456

---

haircut. Then

1642

Sandy has moved away, therefore I seldom see him.

_____

1643

---

houses, barns, trees,

1829

My mother never irons sheets or towels or pillow cases.

1830

No

2016

Underline the correct word:

(*It's, Its*) meal is ready.

2017

---

b

2203

---

a. **This tree was planted by my** *grandfather.*
b. **This tree was planted by** *grandfather* **Resnick.**

In which sentence should *grandfather* be capitalized? ___

2204

Have, heard 141	**Your parents might be expecting you early.** 142

Fill in the two missing forms:

are, been

FORMS OF *BE:* **is, _____, are—was, _____, been.**

329   330

SIMPLE PAST   PAST WITH HELPER

b

played   **(have) played**
cooked   **(has) cooked**
marched   **(had) marched**

These are all regular verbs. Do we use the same form with
or without the helper **have, has,** or **had?** (*Yes, No*)

517   518

Use the verb **set** only when you mention the "something"
that is put or placed somewhere.

No

       a. **I . . . my package on the next seat.**
       b. **I . . . in the same seat all semester.**

In which sentence would **set** be correct? _____

705   706

Underline the subject with one line and the verb with two
lines:

<u>were keys</u>

       How much (*is, are*) **those notebooks?**

893   894

---

       a. **We didn't scarcely have time to eat.**
       b. **We scarcely had time to eat.**

scarcely

Which sentence is wrong because it contains a double neg-

ative? _____

1081   *page 283*   1082

us 1269	Give the ticket to Rex because he likes hockey more than (*I, me*). 1270
No 1456	**Jack walked down the aisle,** *looking for his friends.* *Looking for his friends,* **Jack walked down the aisle.** Can an –*ing* word group be moved from one position to another? (*Yes, No*) 1457
away. Therefore 1643	If there were one tack on the Sahara Desert, Pete would probably step on it. _____ 1644
No commas 1830	The train rumbled to a stop backed up a few yards and stopped again. 1831
Its 2017	To show ownership, use the word (*it's, its*). 2018
b 2204	**One of my** *cousins* **arrived with** *uncle* **Perry.** The word that should be capitalized is (*cousins, uncle*). 2205

might be expecting 142	**Must we wait for Don?** 143
am, were 330	Fill in the two missing forms: **FORMS OF** *BE:* _____, am, are—_____, were, been 331
Yes 518	To make some verbs show past time, we do not add –*d* or –*ed*. Instead, we must change the spelling of the word itself. PRESENT: I *see* **my cousins every day.** SIMPLE PAST: I *saw* **my cousins last week.** The simple past form of *see* is _____. 519
a 706	In this and the following frames, underline the correct forms of **sit** and **set:** **I will** (*sit, set*) **wherever you** (*sit, set*) **the chair.** 707
<u>are</u> notebooks 894	In this and the following frames, underline the verb or words that agree with the subject. In each sentence you will find the verb ahead of the subject. **There** (*was, were*) **several leaks in our tent.** 895
a 1082	In this and the following frames, underline the correct word. To make good sense in several of the sentences you will need to choose a negative word, but remember to avoid double negatives. **I couldn't find my report card** (*anywhere, nowhere*). 1083

I	The dog's constant barking annoyed our neighbors as much as (*we, us*).
1270	1271

Yes	a. **We stood at the window.** b. *We* *watched* the parade. **We stood at the window,** *watching the parade.* To change sentence *b* to an *–ing* word group, we drop the subject *We* and change the verb *watched* to _____.
1457	1458

Correct	An elephant is unable to jump, it can't get its four feet off the ground at the same time. _____
1644	1645

stop, yards,	Wind rain ice rivers and streams are constantly changing the earth's surface.
1831	1832

its	a. you're they're who's it's b. your their whose its Which group contains words that you can use to take the place of a pronoun and its verb? ____
2018	2019

Uncle	When **Mother, Father, Dad,** and so forth, are used as personal names, they are often capitalized.
	     Is *Mother* **calling me?** **What did** *Father* **say?**
	In the sentence below, which italicized word is used in place of a personal name? _____
	     I introduced *Father* **to Nancy's** *mother.*

2205	2206

Must, wait 143	Uncle Ernie must have missed the train. 144

is, was
 	
331
	Other verbs can be used as linking verbs. Some are
	    seem **feel** **become**
	    look **appear** **get** (when it means **become**)
	
	        The children ... tired.
	
	Would each of these verbs fit into the above sentence?
	(*Yes, No*)
	
	332

saw 519	SIMPLE PAST: I *saw* **that movie.** PAST WITH HELPER: I *have seen* **that movie.** Do we use the same form of the verb after the helper *have* that we use for the simple past? (*Yes, No*) 520
sit, set 707	(*Sit, Set*) **your work aside and** (*sit, set*) **down for a rest.** 708
were 895	Here (*are, is*) **the paints for the posters.** 896
anywhere 1083	Dick (*hasn't, has*) **never ridden a horse.** 1084

us 1271	I can't print as neatly as (*he, him*). 1272
watching 1458	Often we can change the first of two sentences to an –*ing* word group. We do this in the same way: a. *We stood at the window.* b. **We watched the parade.** ↓ _____ *at the window,* **we watched the parade.** 1459
jump. It 1645	If you eat a good breakfast, then you won't get hungry before lunch time. _____ 1646
Wind, rain, ice, rivers, 1832	The house and the garage and the fence all needed painting. 1833
a 2019	In this and the following frames, underline the correct word in each pair. Choose the contraction with an apostrophe only when you can fit two words in its place. **I'll get** (*your, you're*) **lunch if** (*your, you're*) **hungry.** 2020
Father 2206	When **mother, father, dad,** and so forth, are used merely to show family relationship, do not capitalize them. *Dad,* **may Jim stay if his** *mother* **says it's all right?** In the sentence above, which italicized word is used to show family relationship? _____ 2207

must have missed 144	I shall be flying to New York at this time tomorrow. 145
Yes 332	The children *seem* tired.　The children *appear* tired. The children *look* tired.　The children *become* tired. The children *feel* tired.　The children *get* tired. In each of these sentences with linking verbs, the adjective **tired** refers back to the subject _____. 333
No 520	PRESENT　　SIMPLE PAST　　PAST WITH HELPER 　see　　　　　saw　　　　　(have) seen We say, "I *saw* that movie," but we say, "I *have* _____ that movie." 521
Set, sit 708	The cat (*sat, set*) waiting for me to (*sit, set*) down its meal. 709
are 896	There (*is, are*) only one thing wrong with our plans. 897
has 1084	The police searched the car very thoroughly, but they found (*something, nothing*). 1085

he

1272

This color suits you better than (*I, me*).

1273

Standing

1459

I heard my name.
Change the above sentence to an *–ing* word group:

_____

1460

Correct

1646

Planets give off no light of their own, they merely reflect the light of the sun.

_____

1647

No commas

1833

Shells tobacco furs and stone are among the many things that have been used for money.

1834

---

your, you're

2020

(*Their, They're*) ripe when (*their, they're*) skin is speckled.

2021

---

mother

2207

When a word such as **mother, father,** or **dad** is used only to show family relationship, it generally follows **a, an, the,** or a possessive word such as **my, his, their,** or **Don's.**

The *mother* of one of the boys asked my *dad* to help.

Should the italicized words be capitalized? (*Yes, No*)

2208

shall be flying 145	**You should have been changing your clothes.** 146
children 333	In the lesson on adjectives that we studied earlier, all the adjectives came *before* the nouns they modified. However, adjectives that are used as subject complements come (*before, after*) the nouns they modify. 334
seen 521	We say, "Cynthia *saw* her grade," but we say, "Cynthia *has* _____ her grade." 522
sat, set 709	**If Mel had (*sat, set*) where he should have (*sat, set*), he would not have been marked absent.** 710
is 897	**Where (*are, is*) my box of tools?** 898
nothing 1085	**The driver didn't see (*any, no*) train coming.** 1086

me 1273	Sandra's parents are not as musical as (*she, her*). 1274
Hearing my name 1460	Earl ran to the door. Change the above sentence to an *–ing* word group: _____ 1461
own. They 1647	Floyd wanted a dollar for the stamp, then he lowered the price to fifty cents. _____ 1648
Shells, tobacco, furs, 1834	A bee is not likely to sting unless it is touched stepped on or molested in some way. 1835
They're, their 2021	(*Whose, Who's*) brother is the boy (*whose, who's*) leading the band? 2022
No 2208	a. **A Father has many responsibilities.** b. **I realize that Father has many responsibilities.** In which sentence should **Father** not be capitalized because it is used only to show family relationship? _____ 2209

Lesson **6** Discovering the Direct Object

[Frames 148-180]

---

after

334

a. **The ride seemed** *long*.
b. **We took a** *long* **ride**.

The adjective *long* is used as a subject complement in

sentence _____.

335

---

seen

522

We *have seen* **many beautiful birds.**

If you dropped the helper *have*, you would need to change

the verb *seen* to _____.

523

---

sat, sat

710

The verbs **rise** and **raise** sometimes cause trouble, too.
To rise means "to go up" or "to get up."
We say, "The fans *rise* from their seats" and "The smoke *rises.*"
Supply the missing verb:

    The river _____ every spring.

711

---

is

898

(*There are, There's*) **no spoons for the ice cream.**

899

---

any

1086

There are many deer in these woods, but we boys didn't see
(*none, any*).

1087

she 1274	We eat our dinner earlier than (*they, them*). 1275
Running to the door 1461	In this and the following frames, combine each pair of sentences by changing the italicized sentence to an *–ing* word group. Write the *–ing* word group in the blank space. **Kip got off the bus.** *He forgot his books.* **Kip got off the bus,** _____**.** 1462
stamp. Then 1648	**The flowers are not real, they are made entirely of glass.** _____ 1649
touched, on, 1835	**Alligators and crocodiles cannot breathe or swallow food under water.** 1836
Whose, who's 2022	(*It's, Its*) **not the same color as** (*its, it's*) **mother.** 2023
a 2209	a. **I often helped Grandfather take care of his garden.** b. **Dan helped his Grandfather take care of his garden.** In which sentence should **Grandfather** not be capitalized because it is used to show family relationship? ____ 2210

Up to this point, all the sentences we have analyzed were

built on a two-part framework: a *subject* and a _____.

---

a

a. **She wore a** *beautiful* **ring.**
b. **The ring looked** *beautiful.*

The adjective *beautiful* is used as a subject complement
in sentence ____.

---

saw

Now we shall look at the three forms of another verb:

PRESENT	SIMPLE PAST	PAST WITH HELPER
do	**did**	**(have) done**

We say, "I *did* the dishes," but we say, "I *have* _____
the dishes."

---

rises

PRESENT	SIMPLE PAST	PAST WITH HELPER
rise (go up)	**rose**	**(have) risen**

We say, "A strong wind *rose*," but we say, "A strong wind

had _____."

There are

How much (*is, are*) **those coats in the window?**

---

any

It must be a poor movie because I met (*nobody, anybody*)
who liked it.

they 1275	The teacher calls on Clark oftener than (*she, her*). 1276
forgetting his books. 1462	*I read over my theme.* **I found several errors.** _____**, I found several errors.** 1463
real. They 1649	The manager didn't know Dad, therefore he wouldn't cash his check. _____ 1650
No commas 1836	Lesson **64** Commas for Interrupters [Frames 1838-1864]
It's, its 2023	(*Whose, Who's*) **going in** (*their, they're*) **car?** 2024
b 2210	**My** *mother* **and** *aunt* **Martha called on Cathy's** *grandmother.* Only one of the italicized words in this sentence should be capitalized. It is the word _____. 2211

verb 148	**The rain <u>stopped</u>.** In this sentence, the action verb **stopped** completes the meaning of the sentence. We feel satisfied because something sensible has been said about the subject _____. 149
b 336	It is easy to tell a subject complement from a direct object. A sentence with a direct object always has an action verb. The action passes from the subject to the direct object. **Earl closed the door.** In this sentence, **Earl** did something to the _____. 337
done 524	We say, "Sally *did* the cooking," but we say, "Sally *has* _____ the cooking." 525
risen 712	Write the correct past forms of **rise:** **The campers** _____ **after the sun** *had* _____. 713
are 900	(*Where are, Where's*) **my other shoes?** 901
nobody 1088	**Dad wouldn't take** (*anything, nothing*) **for his bad cough.** 1089

| her | (*My mother, My mother she*) **bakes wonderful pies.** |
| 1276 | 1277 |

| Reading over my theme, | **Chuck swung at the ball.** *He missed it by a foot.*

Chuck swung at the ball, _____. |
| 1463 | 1464 |

| Dad. Therefore | Lesson **57** Spotting Sentence Errors

[Frames 1652-1671] |
| 1650 | |

| | We sometimes interrupt a sentence to put in one or more words for clearness or emphasis. These words are less important than the rest of the sentence.

The snow, *however*, **soon melted.**

Which word could you omit without changing the meaning of this sentence? _____ |
| | 1838 |

| Who's, their | (*Your, You're*) **stepping on** (*its, it's*) **tail.** |
| 2024 | 2025 |

	Capitalize the first word and all important words in titles of books, stories, poems, plays, and so forth. *The Jinx Ship* "The Ransom of Red Chief" *The Mysterious Island* "The Last Leaf" Write only the capital letters you would use in writing this title: *the blazed trail.* _____
Aunt	
2211	2212

rain 149	**The <u>rain</u> <u>stopped</u> the game.** Here the subject and verb alone do not tell the whole story. In this sentence we are told *what* the rain **stopped**. The meaning of this sentence is not completed until we get to the noun _____. 150
door 337	Now let's look at a sentence with a subject complement: **Earl is chairman.** Did **Earl** do something to the **chairman?** (*Yes, No*) 338
done 525	**Jack** *had done* **every problem.** If you dropped the helper *had,* you would need to change the verb *done* to _____. 526
rose, risen 713	**To raise** means "to lift *something* up." **We** *raised* **the windows to let in some air.** What is the "something" that we raised? _____ 714
Where are 901	(*Here are, Here's*) **the names of our members.** 902
anything 1089	**My throat was so sore that I** (*couldn't, could*) **hardly swallow.** 1090

My mother 1277	(*I and my friend, My friend and I*) had just gone in swimming. 1278
missing it by a foot. 1464	*We walked along the shore.* We picked up interesting shells. _____, we picked up interesting shells. 1465
	In this and the following frames, one of the two items is wrong because it is a run-on sentence or because it contains a fragment. Write the letter of the *correct* item. a. We climbed the tower. And looked at the scenery. b. We climbed the tower and looked at the scenery. _____ 1652
however 1838	The snow, *however*, soon melted. Words like *however* are called interrupters because they break into and interrupt the sentence. If you omit an interrupter, you do not change the meaning of a sentence. Underline the two-word interrupter in this sentence: Nancy, of course, was surprised. 1839
You're, its 2025	(*Its, It's*) color shows that (*its, it's*) ripe. 2026
T B T 2212	a. *The Bottle Imp* b. *the Bottle Imp* c. *The bottle imp* Which story title is correctly capitalized? _____ 2213

game 150	a. The <u>rain</u> <u>stopped</u>. b. The <u>rain</u> <u>stopped</u> the game. In which sentence does the action start with the **rain** and pass over to something else? ____ 151
No 338	a. Earl is chairman. b. Earl is capable. In each of these sentences, the subject complement *refers back* to the subject _____. 339
did 526	Here are the three forms of our third verb: PRESENT SIMPLE PAST PAST WITH HELPER **go** **went** **(have) gone** Write the correct forms of **go**: **This explorer** _____ **where few others** *have* _____. 527
windows 714	**To raise** means "to lift *something* up." Never use the verb **raise** unless you mention the "something" that is lifted. **The passing cars** *raise* **much dust.** What is the "something" that the passing cars raise? ____ 715
Here are 902	Lesson **30** **Subject-Verb Agreement in a Story** [Frames 904-915]
could 1090	**Virginia left the store without buying because** (*either, neither*) **of the two dresses she liked fitted her.** 1091

My friend and I

1278

(*Those, Them*) **are the only ones I like.**

1279

Walking along
the shore,

1465

Earl was on a ladder. *He was washing a window.*

Earl was on a ladder, _____.

1466

---

b

1652

Continue to write the letter of the correct item:

  a. **Clyde was out of breath, he had been running.**
  b. **Clyde was out of breath. He had been running.**

___

1653

---

of course

1839

Nancy, *of course,* **was surprised.**
Nancy was surprised.

Does omitting the interrupter *of course* change the meaning of this sentence? (*Yes, No*)

1840

Its, it's

2026

(*Their, They're*) **not sure** (*who's, whose*) **fingerprints they are.**

2027

---

a

2213

Unless they are the first word in a title, do not capitalize:

SPECIAL ADJECTIVES: **a, an, the**
CONJUNCTIONS: **and, but, or**
SHORT PREPOSITIONS: **of, in, to, for, with,** and so forth

Underline the words you would capitalize in the following title: "**the hunting of the snark.**"

2214

The <u>rain stopped</u> the game.

The **rain** performs the action, and the _____ receives the action.

---

a. ⌒⟶

b. ⟵⌒

One arrow goes from left to right. The other goes from right to left.

Which arrow would represent a sentence with a subject complement? ____

Write the correct past forms of **go:**

I _____ **to find out where Steve** *had* _____.

When you **raise** the flag, the flag **rises.**

The flag **rises** because you _____ it.

Each sentence of the incident that follows presents a problem in subject-verb agreement. Underline the verb that agrees with its subject.

There (*is, are*) **several very young children on our block.**

We (*could, couldn't*) **scarcely hear the announcement this morning.**

Those 1279	Could you do (*them*, *those*) **problems for today?** 1280
washing a window. 1466	*Dad backed his car.* **He struck a post.** _____**, Dad struck a post.** 1467
b 1653	a. **My dad has been an engineer for almost twenty years.** b. **My dad has been an engineer. For almost twenty years.** ____ 1654
No 1840	**Nancy,** *of course,* **was surprised.** In speaking this sentence, you drop your voice when you say *of course* and pause before and after this expression. In writing, you show these pauses by using _____. 1841
They're, whose 2027	Lesson **71** How to Punctuate Quotations [Frames 2029-2055]
"The Hunting . . . Snark" 2214	Copy and capitalize this title: **"turkey in the straw"** _____ 2215

game	The <u>driver</u> <u>stopped</u> the car. Here the **driver** performs the action, and the _____ receives the action.
152	153

b	In this and the following frames, one sentence contains a direct object and the other a subject complement.
	
	      a. **The teacher praised the** *winner*.
	      b. **My best friend was the** *winner*.
	
	Which sentence contains a subject complement? ____

340	341

went, gone	**All the lights** *went* **out.** If you added the helper *have* to the verb, you would need to change *went* to _____.
528	529

raise	Here are the forms of the verb **raise:** PRESENT SIMPLE PAST PAST WITH HELPER **raise** (to lift) **raised** **(have) raised** The simple past form and the form we use with *have, has,* or *had* are (*alike, different*).
716	717

are	**One of these children** (*has, have*) **a very annoying habit.**
904	905

could	**Arthur wouldn't discuss his plans with** (*nobody, anybody*).
1092	1093

those 1280	Mr. Osgood asked (*we, us*) boys to give his car a push. 1281
Backing his car, 1467	I sat on the dock. *I dangled my legs over the edge.* I sat on the dock, _____ _____. 1468
a 1654	a. The sky was cloudy, therefore the eclipse was not visible. b. The sky was cloudy. Therefore the eclipse was not visible. ____ 1655

commas
 	
1841
	The commas around an interrupter help your reader to keep his mind on the main idea of the sentence.
	
	    a. Frank went by the way to Washington.
	    b. Frank went, by the way, to Washington.
	
	In which sentence is it easier to follow the main idea? ____
	
	1842

	To quote means "to repeat someone's words." Around the dinner table, you might quote, or repeat, what a friend, a teacher, or the newspaper said. The repeated words are called a **quotation.** To quote a person means to _____ what he said. 2029
"Turkey in the Straw" 2215	Copy and capitalize this title: "the house on the hill" _____ 2216

car 153	The <u>police</u> <u>stopped</u> the fight. Here the _____ perform the action, and the _____ receives the action. 154
b 341	a. **The strawberries look** *ripe*. b. **The sparks started a** *fire*. Which sentence contains a subject complement? ____ 342

gone
 	
529
	Verbs like **see, do,** and **go** are called **irregular verbs** because they do not follow the *–ed* pattern of most verbs.
	
	    a. **take write drive speak**
	    b. **bake travel change wait**
	
	Which group consists of irregular verbs? ____
	
	530

alike 717	Now let's compare the two verbs: PRESENT SIMPLE PAST PAST WITH HELPER **rise** (to go up) **rose** (have) **risen** **raise** (to lift) **raised** (have) **raised** Which verb is regular? _____ 718
has 905	**Little Bobby Klieg** (*don't, doesn't*) **know that he should not take things that do not belong to him.** 906
anybody 1093	# Lesson 37 Unit Review [Frames 1095-1115]

us 1281	(*We, Us*) **girls baked all the cookies for the party.** 1282
dangling my legs over the edge. 1468	*He picked up his bat.* **He walked to the plate.** _____**, he walked to the plate.** 1469
b 1655	a. **There was one good feature about the movie. It finally ended.** b. **There was one good feature about the movie, it finally ended.** ____ 1656
b 1842	Here are some common interrupters that should be fenced off by commas from the rest of the sentence: **however for example I suppose** **of course on the whole if possible** Punctuate this sentence: **The sandwiches for example cost twenty cents.** 1843

repeat (tell)
 	
2029
	When you repeat what a person said directly *in his own words*, you are making a **direct quotation.**
	    a. **The teacher said, "Your work has improved."**
	    b. **The teacher said that my work has improved.**
	In which sentence do you find the *actual* words that the teacher used? ____
	
	2030

"The House on the Hill" 2216	Capitalize, too, the titles of movies, works of art, pieces of music, and so forth. **"No Time for Sergeants"** **"Home on the Range"** **"Woman with Chrysanthemums"** **"Waltz of the Flowers"** Write only the capital letters you would use in writing this movie title: **"the legend of lobo."** _____ 2217

police, fight	Any word that receives the action of the verb is called a **direct object.** It is called a *direct* object because it receives the action of the verb *directly* from the subject. **The rain stopped the game.** The direct object of the action verb **stopped** is the noun _____.
154	155

a	a. **The lifeguard rescued the** *swimmer.* b. **Tom is an excellent** *swimmer.* Which sentence contains a subject complement? ____
342	343

a	a. saw did went b. seen done gone Which group of verbs would you use to show simple past time when the helping verb **have, has,** or **had** is *not* present? ____
530	531

raise	Use the verb **raise** only when you mention the "something" that is lifted up. a. **The price of our paper ... this year.** b. **We ... the price of our paper this year.** In which sentence would **raised** be correct? ____
718	719

doesn't	**Any article, like a book or a sweater, often** (*disappears, disappear*) **if it is left on the porch.**
906	907

	Underline the correct word or words in each frame: **Everything Linda does, she does** (*perfect, perfectly*).
	1095

We 1282	Why don't you let (*we, us*) fellows help you? 1283
Picking up his bat, 1469	**Shep came to the door.** *He was wagging his tail.* **Shep came to the door,** _____. 1470
a 1656	a. **A deer nudged the hunter, who had fallen asleep on a log.** b. **A deer nudged the hunter. Who had fallen asleep on a log.** ____ 1657

sandwiches,
example,
 	
1843
	INTERRUPTERS: **however for example I suppose**
	                     of course on the whole if possible
	Punctuate this sentence:
	
	      Earl I suppose took all the credit.
	
	1844

a
 	
2030
	When you repeat what a person said indirectly in *your* words, not his words, you are making an **indirect quotation.**
	    a. **The teacher said, "Your work has improved."**
	    b. **The teacher said that my work has improved.**
	In which sentence is the teacher's remark repeated in *someone else's* words? ____
	
	2031

T L L 2217	a. **"On top of old Smoky"** b. **"On Top Of Old Smoky"** c. **"On Top of Old Smoky"** Which song title is capitalized correctly? ____ 2218

The rain stopped the *game*.

In this sentence, the subject and verb alone do not express the complete idea. The meaning is not completed until we add the direct object *game*.

We say, therefore, that this sentence has a (*two-part, three-part*) framework.

game

155

156

---

b

Find the subject, verb, and subject complement in each sentence and write them in the proper blanks:

The first boat was probably a log.

S   V   SC

_____   _____   _____

343

344

---

a

a. I *done* my work.   We *seen* the accident.
b. I *did* my work.   We *saw* the accident.

Which pair of sentences is correct? ____

531

532

---

b

a. **Many pupils ... their hands when the teacher asked for volunteers.**
b. **Many pupils' hands ... when the teacher asked for volunteers.**

In which sentence would **raised** be correct? ____

719

720

---

disappears

When a garden tool or an article of clothing (*is, are***) missing, one immediately thinks of little Bobby.**

907

908

---

perfectly

Skippy barked (*angry, angrily***) at his reflection in the mirror.**

1095

1096

us 1283	**(We, Us) citizens must not fail to vote.** Note to student: You are now ready for Unit Test 6, to be followed by the Halfway Test. 1284
wagging his tail. 1470	*Maxine excused herself politely.* **She went to her room.** _____**, Maxine went to her room.** 1471
a 1657	a. **We visited Mount Vernon. The home of George Washington.** b. **We visited Mount Vernon, the home of George Washington.** ____ 1658

Earl, suppose,
 	
 1844
	When an interrupter comes at the beginning or end of a sentence, only one comma is needed to set it off.
	
	     a. *However* **the rain didn't stop the game.**
	     b. **The rain** *however* **didn't stop the game.**
	
	 Which sentence requires only one comma? ____ 1845

b 2031	A quotation that repeats a person's exact words is called (*a direct, an indirect*) quotation. 2032
c 2218	In this and the following frames, copy only the words to which capitals should be added, and write them with capitals. (Several uses of capitals from the preceding lessons are included.) **It was officer Schultz who ticketed the judge's car.** 2219

three-part 156	Cliff painted the boat. **Cliff** got a bucket of paint and a brush and performed an action. He painted something—the **boat**. In this sentence, as in the previous ones, the direct object (**boat**) _____ the action of the verb. 157
S V SC boat was log 344	**This mattress feels too soft.** S V SC _____ _____ _____ 345
b 532	Write the correct past forms of **see:** **The shoplifter** _____ **that the store detective** *had* _____ **him.** 533
a 720	In this and the following frames, underline the correct verb: **The man** (*rose, raised*) **and offered the lady his seat.** 721
is 908	**Every now and then, one of the neighbors** (*come, comes*) **to the door to inquire for a lost article.** 909
angrily 1096	**Our argument now seems rather** (*foolish, foolishly*) **to both of us.** 1097

We

1284

Lesson 44 Meet the Adverb Clause

[Frames 1286-1316]

Excusing herself
politely,

1471

Lesson 51 Using Appositives to Combine Sentences

[Frames 1473-1500]

---

b

1658

a. Mr. Wetherby makes appointments. Then he forgets to keep them.
b. Mr. Wetherby makes appointments, then he forgets to keep them.

_____

1659

---

a

1845

Here are other expressions often used as interrupters:

after all	to tell the truth
it seems	on the other hand
by the way	as a matter of fact

Punctuate this sentence:

The other driver it seems didn't see the light.

1846

---

a direct

2032

a. The teacher said, "Your work has improved."
b. The teacher said that my work has improved.

Only one of these sentences repeats the exact words of the teacher.

Which sentence contains a *direct* quotation? ____

2033

Officer

2219

Have you heard that umpire Henrikson was hit by a ball in friday's game?

_____

2220

receives 157	Instead of receiving the action, the direct object sometimes shows the *result* of an action. **Cliff built a boat.** In this sentence, **Cliff** didn't do something to a boat that was already there. Rather, the *result of his action* was a _____. 158
S V mattress feels SC soft 345	**His brother became a very good doctor.** S V SC _____ _____ _____ 346
saw, seen 533	Write the correct past forms of **see**: **If John** *had* _____ **the accident that I** _____**, he would drive more carefully.** 534
rose 721	**I** (*rose, raised*) **the cover and peeked into the box.** 722
comes 909	**Sometimes Mr. and Mrs. Klieg** (*recognizes, recognize*) **an article and take it back to its owner.** 910
foolish 1097	**The kitchen sink was leaking** (*bad, badly*). 1098

I awoke *early*.

The word *early* is an adverb because it modifies the verb **awoke**.

The adverb **early** answers the question (*When? Where? How?*).

1286

Ritzi eats too much.

Do you know whether **Ritzi** is a boy, a girl, a dog, or an elephant? (*Yes, No*)

1473

---

a

1659

---

a. **This machine weighs the eggs. And sorts them according to size.**
b. **This machine weighs the eggs and sorts them according to size.**

_____

1660

---

driver, seems,

1846

INTERRUPTERS: **after all**   **to tell the truth**
                       it seems   **on the other hand**
                       by the way   **as a matter of fact**

Punctuate this sentence:

   My father on the other hand is very patient.

1847

---

a

2033

---

a. **Tommy said that he wouldn't eat spinach.**
b. **Tommy said, "I won't eat spinach."**

Which sentence contains a *direct* quotation? _____

2034

Umpire, Friday's

2220

The chairman introduced professor Mary Arkwright of Leonia university.

_____

2221

boat 158	Now we are ready to complete our definition of the direct object: A **direct object** receives the action of the verb or shows the _____ of this action. 159
S V brother became SC doctor 346	**The owner of the other car got angry.** S V SC _____ _____ _____ 347
seen, saw 534	Write the correct past forms of **do**: **Dr. Robbins** _____ **what most doctors would** *have* _____. 535
raised 722	**Traffic deaths have** (*raised, risen*) **greatly in recent years.** 723
recognize 910	**However, there** (*are, is*) **always many unclaimed articles in their garage.** 911
badly 1098	**The growth of these trees is very** (*rapid, rapidly*). 1099

a. I awoke *early*.
b. I awoke *when the alarm rang.*

In sentence *a*, the adverb *early* answers the question *When?*

In sentence *b*, a group of words answers the question *When?*

These words are _____.

1286   1287

No

Ritzi, *our* <u>cat</u>**, eats too much.**

Now you know that **Ritzi** is a cat.

The noun *cat* explains the noun _____.

1473   1474

---

b

a. **Some plants grow best in the sun, others do better in the shade.**
b. **Some plants grow best in the sun. Others do better in the shade.**

____

1660   1661

---

father, hand,

If a group of words cannot be omitted from a sentence, it is not an interrupter.

    a. **I was shocked** *by the way* **he drove.**
    b. **He drove** *by the way* **very recklessly.**

By the way is an interrupter in only one of these sentences. Which sentence requires commas? ____

1847   1848

---

b

    a. **Tommy said that he wouldn't eat spinach.**
    b. **Tommy said, "I won't eat spinach."**

Quotation marks ("—") are used only around the (*direct, indirect*) quotation.

2034   2035

Professor, University

For my birthday this spring Ralph's aunt gave me a copy of *a boy on horseback.*

_____

2221   2222

result 159	The usual position of a **direct object** is (*before, after*) the action verb. 160
S V SC owner got angry 347	A subject complement always refers back to the _____ of the sentence. 348
did, done 535	Write the correct past forms of **do**: I _____ **the same problem that Sue** *had* _____. 536
risen 723	**You must have** (*risen, rose*) **early to catch all those fish.** 724
are 911	**Bobby's mother and father** (*tries, try*) **to explain to him that he must not bring home other people's belongings.** 912
rapid 1099	**Brush your teeth** (*good, well*) **after eating sweets.** 1100

a. **I awoke** *early*.
b. **I awoke** *when the alarm rang*.

The word group *when the alarm rang* in sentence *b* does the same job that the adverb _____ does in sentence *a*.

1288

---

a. **Pete has just started school.**
b. **Pete,** *my youngest brother*, **has just started school.**

Which sentence is clearer? ____

1475

---

a. **The strike was finally settled. The men went back to work.**
b. **The strike was finally settled, the men went back to work.**

____

1662

We sometimes start a sentence with the word **Yes, No, Well,** or **Why.** Put a comma after one of these words when it is not a necessary part of the sentence.

    a. *No* **the Wellers are not planning to move.**
    b. *No* **money is needed for this hobby.**

From which sentence could *No* be omitted? ____

1849

Let's see how a direct quotation is punctuated:

    The teacher said, "Your work has improved."

The two pairs of quotation marks ("—") go around (*the entire sentence, only the quoted words*).

2036

My father is younger than uncle Bert.

_____

2223

after 160	Here is how to tell when a sentence has a direct object: If, for example, the verb is the word *returned*, ask yourself, "Returned *what?*" or "Returned *whom?*" If you see a word that answers this question, it is a *direct object*. **The <u>wind</u> <u>rattled</u> the windows of the old house.** "Rattled *what?*" _____ (one word) 161
subject 348	Can both nouns and adjectives serve as subject complements? (*Yes, No*) 349
did, done 536	Write the correct past forms of **go:** **Dick** _____ **downstairs to see if the company** *had* _____. 537
risen 724	a. **lie sit rise** b. **lay set raise** Which group of words would you use to show that you are changing the position of something? ____ 725
try 912	**A scolding or a spanking** (*seems, seem*) **to do no good.** 913
well 1100	**I couldn't see** (*good, well*) **in the darkness.** 1101

early

1288

I awoke *when the* <u>alarm</u> <u>rang</u>*.*

Look at just the italicized word group. It has both a subject and a verb.

The subject is *alarm,* and the verb is _____ .

1289

---

b

1475

---

a. **Pete has just started school.**
b. **Pete,** *my youngest* <u>brother</u>**, has just started school.**

Sentence *b* is clearer because the noun _____ explains who **Pete** is.

1476

---

a

1662

---

a. **Astronomers can tell what each star is made of. By its color.**
b. **Astronomers can tell what each star is made of by its color.**

_____

1663

---

a

1849

---

a. *No* **the Wellers are not planning to move.**
b. *No* **money is needed for this hobby.**

In which sentence would you put a comma after *No?* _____

1850

---

only the quoted words

2036

The **he said** (or similar expression) can be put either before or after the quotation.

a. *The teacher said,* **"Your work has improved."**
b. **"Your work has improved,"** *said the teacher.*

The **he said** expression comes after the quotation in sentence _____ .

2037

Uncle

2223

The principal of Leland Junior high school got captain Baker to speak to the graduating class.

_____

2224

windows 161	The wind rattled the windows of the old house. The noun **windows** is a *direct* _____. 162
Yes 349	Lesson **12** **Prepositions Show Relationships** [Frames 351-376]
went, gone 537	Write the correct past forms of **go**: **You should** *have* _____ **where Sandy** _____. 538
b 725	Lesson **24** **Supplying the Right Verb Forms** [Frames 727-750]
seems 913	Recently, Mrs. Klieg got a good idea. On her gate she now posts a sign which says, "The following articles (*was, were*) recently brought home by Bobby. Do any of them belong to you?" 914
well 1101	Harvey's work in math was always (*good, well*). 1102

rang 1289	*when the alarm rang* Although this word group has a subject and a verb, can it stand by itself as a complete sentence? *(Yes, No)* 1290
brother 1476	**Pete,** *my youngest brother,* **has just started school.** A noun (or pronoun) set *after* another noun (or pronoun) to explain it is called an **appositive.** In the above sentence, the word used as an appositive is the noun _____. 1477
b 1663	a. **Arlene lost my address, therefore she didn't write me.** b. **Arlene lost my address. Therefore she didn't write me.** _____ 1664
a 1850	a. *Why* **won't the car start?** b. *Why* **the car was hardly moving at all.** In which sentence could you omit *Why* without changing the meaning? _____ 1851
b 2037	a. *The teacher said,* **"Your work has improved."** b. **"Your work has improved,"** *said the teacher.* In both sentences, the quotation is separated from the rest of the sentence by a *(period, comma)*. 2038
High School, Captain 2224	**A book that has been translated into russian, japanese, and numerous other foreign languages is Mark Twain's** *the Adventures of Tom Sawyer.* _____ 2225

object	The <u>police</u> soon <u>found</u> the lost child. "Found *whom*?" _____ (one word)
162	163

	bee table These nouns give you the picture of two separate, unrelated things. For all you know, could the **table** be in Chicago and the **bee** in China? (*Yes, No*)
	351

gone, went	Lesson **18** *Come, Run, and Give* [Frames 540-566]
538	

	In this story of a true experience, write the correct past form of each verb in parentheses. One evening when Grandfather Brooks _____ (*come*) over to see them, Mr. and Mrs. Doty asked him if he would baby-sit with their six-month-old daughter while they went to a movie.
	727

were	It is not unusual to see a person stop to read the list and exclaim, "(*Here's, Here are*) my lost rubbers at last!"
914	915

good	Our church looks (*nice, nicely*) at Christmas time.
1102	1103

No 1290	*when the <u>alarm</u> <u>rang</u>* A word group that has a subject and a verb but cannot stand by itself is called a **clause.** Do both a sentence and a clause have a subject and a verb? (*Yes, No*) 1291
brother 1477	**Pete,** *my youngest <u>brother</u>*, **has just started school.** An appositive usually has words that modify it. The two words that modify the appositive *brother* are _____ and _____. 1478
b 1664	a. **Phil stood in line, hoping to get a ticket.** b. **Phil stood in line. Hoping to get a ticket.** _____ 1665
b 1851	a. *Why* **won't the car start?** b. *Why* **the car was hardly moving at all.** In which sentence would you put a comma after *Why?* _____ 1852
comma 2038	Add the missing comma: **The coach said "Stand closer to the plate."** 2039
Russian, Japanese, The 2225	**Both my mother and aunt Shirley belong to the Schubert music club.** _____ 2226

child 163	The <u>police</u> soon <u>found</u> the lost child. The noun **child** is a _____ _____. 164
Yes 351	bee . ? . table If there is a relationship between these two things, there is no word to tell you what it is. Underline three words that you could put between **bee** and **table** to show what their relationship might be: **on can near big over soon** 352
	In this lesson we study three more little verbs that we use many times each day: **come, run,** and **give.** To show simple past time, do we add *–d* or *–ed* to these verbs? (*Yes, No*) 540
came 727	**Grandfather Brooks** _____ (*see*) **that they were eager to go; so he consented to stay.** 728
Here are 915	Lesson **31** Unit Review [Frames 917-945]
nice 1103	**Jimmy looked** (*sad, sadly*) **at his broken balloon.** 1104

Yes	Both a sentence and a clause have a subject and a verb. The important difference between them is that a clause (*can, cannot*) stand by itself.
1291	1292
my, youngest	**Pete,** *my youngest brother*, **has just started school.** An appositive with its modifying words is set off from the rest of the sentence by _____.
1478	1479
a	a. **Although our school is large. The students are very friendly.** b. **Although our school is large, the students are very friendly.** _____
1665	1666
b	Punctuate this sentence: **Well we can't expect to win every game.**
1852	1853
said,	Add the missing comma: **"Stand closer to the plate" said the coach.**
2039	2040
Aunt, Music Club	**Do you know that grandfather Reese was once the football coach at Ridley college?** _____
2226	2227

direct object	If the sentence has no word that answers a question like "Returned *what?*" or "Found *whom?*" the sentence has no direct object.
	a. <u>Frank</u> <u><u>returned</u></u> very soon.
	b. <u>Frank</u> <u><u>returned</u></u> my book.
164	Which sentence answers "Returned *what?*" _____ 165

on, near, over	bee .?. table
	Underline three other words that you could put between **bee** and **table** to show what their relationship might be:
	did by under is beside must
352	353

No	PRESENT SIMPLE PAST PAST WITH HELPER
	come came (have) come
	run ran (have) run
	give gave (have) given
	These three verbs are (*regular, irregular*).
540	541

saw	Soon after they had _____ (*go*), the baby _____ (*begin*) **to cry.**
728	729

	Use the verb **don't** only where you can substitute the words (*do not, does not*).
	917

sadly	**Onions taste** (*different, differently*) **when they're cooked.**
1104	1105

cannot 1292	**I awoke** *when the alarm rang.* A clause that does the work of an adverb is called an **adverb clause**. The clause *when the alarm rang* is therefore an _____ *clause.* 1293
commas 1479	Here is the appositive with its modifiers by itself: *my youngest brother* Does an appositive, like a clause, have both a subject and a verb? (*Yes, No*) 1480
b 1666	a. **A cat seldom gives up a bad habit that it is allowed to form.** b. **A cat seldom gives up a bad habit. That it is allowed to form.** _____ 1667
Well, 1853	Punctuate this sentence: **Yes I did wipe my feet on the mat.** 1854
plate, 2040	Look at the three places where a comma or period and quotation marks come together in these sentences: a. **The coach said, "Stand closer to the plate."** b. **"Stand closer to the plate," said the coach.** The period and the comma always come (*before, after*) the quotation marks. 2041
Grandfather, College 2227	**My uncle sang "a visit from St. Nicholas" for the children at the Parkside hospital just before christmas.** _____ 2228

b 165	a. **Frank** <u>returned</u> very soon. b. **Frank** <u>returned</u> my book. Which sentence contains a direct object?____ 166
by, under, beside 353	**bee** *on* **table** **bee** *by* **table** **bee** *near* **table** **bee** *under* **table** **bee** *over* **table** **bee** *beside* **table** By using different words, we change the *re*_____ between **bee** and **table**. 354
irregular 541	PRESENT SIMPLE PAST PAST WITH HELPER **come** **came** **(have) come** The simple past form of **come** is _____. 542
gone, began 729	**He** _____ (*give*) **the baby her bottle of milk, which she** _____ (*drink*) **very hungrily.** 730
do not 917	Suppose that a sentence has a singular subject. If this singular subject is followed by a prepositional phrase with a plural object, the verb should be (*singular, plural*). 918
different 1105	**I felt the edge of the knife very** (*cautious, cautiously*). 1106

adverb
 	
1293
	Adverb clauses, just like adverbs, can answer other questions about verbs, too.
	
	    a. **We stopped** *there.*
	    b. **We stopped** *where the* <u>*road*</u> <u>*turns.*</u>
	
	Both the adverb *there* in *a* and the adverb clause in *b* answer the question (*When? Where? How?*). 1294

No 1480	An appositive can come at the end of a sentence as well as in the middle. **The Eiffel Tower in Paris was built by Alexandre Eiffel,** *a French engineer.* The appositive that explains who **Alexandre Eiffel** was is the noun _____. 1481
a 1667	a. **Harold offered to do the job. Then he tried to get out of doing it.** b. **Harold offered to do the job, then he tried to get out of doing it.** ____ 1668
Yes, 1854	In this and the following frames, add the necessary commas. The number after each sentence shows how many commas are needed. **Our next meeting by the way is on Tuesday. (2)** 1855
before 2041	Take a long, hard look at these punctuation marks, and make a mental picture of them: ,"_____." When a comma or period and quotation marks come together, always put the comma or period (*first, last*). 2042
"A Visit ..." Hospital, Christmas 2228	Lesson **78** Unit Review

Frank <u>returned</u> very soon.

b

Frank himself returned. He didn't return something else, like a book or a bicycle or money.

Does this sentence contain a direct object? (*Yes, No*).

166 | 167

---

relationship

Now instead of having two nouns, we shall have a verb and a noun.

skated   park

Do you see any word that shows you the relationship between the verb **skated** and the noun **park?** (*Yes, No*)

354 | 355

---

came

Write the simple past form of **come:**

Your letter _____ yesterday.

542 | 543

---

gave, drank

After the baby had _____ (*fall*) asleep, Grandfather **Brooks went downstairs to read the paper.**

730 | 731

---

singular

In a sentence that begins with **There is, There are, Here is,** or **Here are,** look for the subject (*before, after*) the verb.

918 | 919

---

cautiously

Which lives (*longer, longest*)—a dog or a cat?

1106 | 1107

Where? 1294	a. **The man greeted us** *warmly*. b. **The man greeted us** *as though <u>he knew</u> us*. Both the adverb *warmly* in sentence *a* and the adverb clause in sentence *b* answer the question (*When? Where? How?*). 1295

engineer
 	
1481
	An appositive always comes *after* (not before) the word it explains.
	
	    a. **Don Sibley, our** *chairman*, **was absent.**
	    b. **Our** *chairman*, **Don Sibley, was absent.**
	
	In which sentence is the noun *chairman* an appositive?
	
	——
	
	1482

a 1668	a. **We didn't buy the car, it had been in a bad accident.** b. **We didn't buy the car. It had been in a bad accident.** —— 1669
meeting, way, 1855	**Aluminum for example is a very soft metal. (2)** 1856
first 2042	Add the missing punctuation: **The teacher said ____ Your work has improved ____** 2043
	In this and the following frames, copy only the words to which capitals should be added, and write them with capitals: **Dean works for the Davis drug company every saturday afternoon.** 2230

No

167

a. **Harold studied his math.**
b. **Harold studied in school.**

Which sentence contains a direct object? _____
The direct object is the noun _____.

168

No

355

skated .?. park

Underline three words that you could put between **skated**
and **park** to show their relationship:

in   again   through   large   around   new

356

---

came

543

PRESENT   SIMPLE PAST   PAST WITH HELPER

come   came   (have) come

Write the two different past forms of **come**:

A storm _____ up before the children *had* _____
home from the park.

544

---

fallen

731

An hour later the baby _____ (*begin*) **to cry again.**

732

---

after

919

The words **There's, Here's,** and **Where's** should be used
only when they are followed by (*singular, plural*) subjects.

920

---

longer

1107

Is it (*cheaper, cheapest*) **to travel by bus, train, or plane?**

1108

How?

1295

No single adverb can answer the question *Why?* An adverb clause, however, can answer this question.

    a. **We hurried** *because* <u>it</u> <u>had</u> <u>started</u> *to rain.*
    b. **We hurried** *after* <u>it</u> <u>had</u> <u>started</u> *to rain.*

In which sentence does the adverb clause answer the question *Why?*

1296

---

a

1482

The Hawaiian Islands were discovered by Captain Cook, an English explorer.

The appositive in this sentence is the noun _____.

1483

---

b

1669

a. **Dan received the Eagle Scout Award. The highest award in scouting.**
b. **Dan received the Eagle Scout Award, the highest award in scouting.**

____

1670

---

aluminum,
example,

1856

Well the concert to tell the truth was disappointing. (3)

1857

The teacher said,
"Your work has
improved."

2043

The teacher said, "Your work has improved."

Like all sentences, this sentence begins with a capital letter. Does the quotation within the sentence also begin with a capital letter? (*Yes, No*)

2044

Drug Company,
Saturday

2230

When my mother was a girl, she lived near some indians in oklahoma.

_____

2231

a math 168	a. <u>Roses</u> <u>grow</u> along the fence. b. The <u>Nortons</u> <u>grow</u> beautiful roses. Which sentence contains a direct object? _____ The direct object is the noun _____. 169
in, through, around 356	skated .?. park Underline three other words that you could put between **skated** and **park** to show their relationship: **toward across tree past last** 357
came, come 544	PRESENT: **The squirrels** *come* **to our porch for food.** If you changed this sentence from present to past, you would need to change the verb *come* to _____. 545
began 732	He _____ (*lay*) aside his paper and _____ (*run*) upstairs to see what the matter was. 733
singular 920	In this and the following frames, underline the verb that agrees with its subject. Remember that if a verb showing present time ends in *s*, it is singular, not plural. **Your height and weight (*are, is*) perfect for football.** 921
cheapest 1108	**The new road is (*more wider, wider*) than the old one.** 1109

a
 	
1296
	An adverb clause can also answer the question *On what condition?*
	
	    a. **I went** *where my friend invited me.*
	    b. **I will go** *if my friend invites me.*
	
	In which sentence does the adverb clause answer the question *On what condition?*
	
	<div align="right">1297</div>

explorer 1483	**In Laredo, a town on the Mexican border, the train stops for customs inspection.** The appositive in this sentence is the noun _____. <div align="right">1484</div>
b 1670	a. **Because they are intelligent. Elephants are easy to train.** b. **Because they are intelligent, elephants are easy to train.** _____ <div align="right">1671</div>
Well, concert, truth, 1857	**Frank I suppose plans to go to summer school. (2)** <div align="right">1858</div>

Yes
 	
2044
	It is easy to see why a quotation should always start with a capital letter. It is the beginning of someone else's sentence even though it may not be the beginning of yours.
	
	    a. **A man called, "Your tire is flat."**
	    b. **A man called, "your tire is flat."**
	
	In which sentence is the capitalization correct? _____
	
	<div align="right">2045</div>

Indians, Oklahoma 2231	**The Pilgrim methodist church was filled to capacity on easter.** _____ <div align="right">2232</div>

b
roses
 	
169
	In this and the following frames, you will find a subject, action verb, and direct object in jumbled order. Put them in sensible order and write them in the proper blanks.
	
	EXAMPLE **melts** **ice** **sun** **milk** **cats** **drink**
	          S V DO S V DO
	    sun melts ice ____ ____ ____
	                                              170

toward, across, past 357	A word that relates a noun or pronoun that follows it to some other word in the sentence is called a **preposition**. A preposition is a word that (*repeats, relates*). 358
came 545	**The mail** *has come* **late this morning.** If you dropped the helper *has*, you would need to change the verb *come* to _____. 546
laid, ran 733	**He found that the baby had** _____ (*throw*) **off her covers.** 734
are 921	**A doctor or a nurse** (*were, was*) **always on hand.** 922
wider 1109	**Flicka, the high-spirited colt, becomes** (*tamer, more tamer*) **at the end of the story.** 1110

b 1297	Here are some adverb clause signals. They are arranged according to the question the clause answers. WHEN? while, when, whenever, as, before, after, since, until WHERE? where, wherever These are the words that (*start, end*) adverb clauses. 1298
town 1484	We often write a sentence that explains *who* or *what* someone or something is in the previous sentence. a. **Mt. Everest is in Tibet.** b. **It is the world's highest mountain.** Sentence *b* explains the noun _____ in sentence *a*. 1485
b 1671	# Lesson 58 Unit Review [Frames 1673-1696]
Frank, suppose, 1858	**Yes our carnival on the whole was very successful. (3)** 1859
a 2045	Now let's check the several points you have just studied about punctuating quotations: a. **The nurse replied, "The patient is feeling better."** b. **The nurse replied "that the patient is feeling better."** Which sentence is correct? ____ 2046
Methodist Church, Easter 2232	**You can see the river from uncle Roy's office in the Chase building.** _____ 2233

page 340

S V DO cats drink milk 170	puzzles enjoy children S V DO _____ _____ _____ 171
relates 358	You can already spell the word *position*. To spell the word *preposition*, you merely write the letters _____ before *position*. 359
came 546	a. **My cousin . . . to visit me.** b. **My cousin *has* . . . to visit me.** In which sentence would *come* be correct? ____ 547
thrown 734	**Grandfather covered the baby snugly and _____ (*sing*) her to sleep.** 735
was 922	**The teacher or a pupil (*read, reads*) the notices.** 923
tamer 1110	**The new model has a (*powerfuller, more powerful*) engine.** 1111

Here are more clause signals:

HOW? **as if, as though**
WHY? **because, since, as, so that**
ON WHAT CONDITION? **if, unless, although, though**

Do some of these clause signals consist of more than one word? (*Yes, No*)

A sentence that identifies a word in the previous sentence can often be changed to an appositive word group.

a. **Mt. Everest is in Tibet.** b. **It is the world's highest mountain.**

Mt. Everest, *the world's highest mountain*, **is in Tibet.**

Which sentence became an appositive word group? ____

In this review lesson you will find the story of an unusual experience. In each frame are two word groups. If the two word groups should be written as a single sentence, put down your answer like this:

EXAMPLE: **The little girl was shy   and clung to her mother.**

shy and   (*Turn to the next frame.*)

Bobby after all is only eight years old. (2)

---

a. "The patient is feeling better" replied the nurse.
b. "The patient is feeling better," replied the nurse.

Which sentence is correct? ____

When it is summer in the united states, it is winter in south america.

_____

S V children enjoy DO puzzles 171	stamps Henry saves S V DO _____ _____ _____ 172
pre 359	**bee** *on* **table** The preposition *on* relates the noun **table** to the word **bee,** which is also a _____. 360
b 547	PRESENT SIMPLE PAST PAST WITH HELPER **run** **ran** **(have) run** The simple past form of **run** is _____. 548
sang 735	**Some time later, when the baby was crying loudly again,** **he** _____ (*bring*) **her downstairs in her basket,** **which he** _____ (*lay*) **on a chair.** 736
reads 923	**Snow and ice** (*cover, covers*) **the Antarctic regions.** 924
more powerful 1111	**It was so dark that we couldn't take** (*no, any*) **pictures.** 1112

Yes 1299	Every adverb clause starts with a clause signal. After this clause signal you will always find a subject and a _____. 1300
b 1486	An identifying sentence usually begins with words such as **It is, He was,** or **They are.** To change such a sentence to an appositive word group, you merely drop these words. **~~It is~~ the world's highest mountain.** This sentence can become an appositive word group if we drop the words _____. 1487
	If the two word groups should be written as two separate sentences, put down your answer like this: EXAMPLE: **I enjoyed the book it was full of surprises.** *book. It* (*Turn to the next frame.*) 1674
Bobby, all, 1860	**Why my mother was very pleased of course with your gift. (3)** 1861
b 2047	a. **"The patient is feeling better," replied the nurse.** b. **"The patient is feeling better", replied the nurse.** Which sentence is correct? ____ 2048
United States, South America 2234	**Both christians and jews celebrate thanksgiving day.** _____ 2235

S V Henry saves DO stamps 172	people lawns water		
	S	V	DO
	_____	_____	_____
			173

---

noun

360

skated _through_ **park**

The preposition _through_ relates the noun **park** to the word **skated**, which is a _____.

361

---

ran

548

Write the simple past form of **run**:

    The truck _____ off the road.

549

---

brought, laid

736

However, nothing that he _____ (do) would stop the baby from crying.

737

---

cover

924

My father or my mother (_wake, wakes_) me for school.

925

---

any

1112

Jerry wouldn't let (_anybody, nobody_) ride his bicycle.

1113

verb 1300	Underline one clause signal that could start an adverb clause that answers the question *When?* while so that because 1301
It is 1487	After we change a sentence to an appositive word group, we put it in the sentence *after* the word it explains. a. **Mt. Everest,** *the world's highest mountain,* **is in Tibet.** b. **Mt. Everest is in Tibet,** *the world's highest mountain.* Which sentence is correct? _____ 1488
	Dad and I like to fish therefore we accepted Uncle John's invitation to use his cabin. _____ (In checking your answers, do not count comma errors. Commas will be studied in the next unit.) 1675
Why, pleased, course, 1861	**The other team it seems was out of practice. (2)** 1862
a 2048	a. **The nurse replied, "The patient is feeling better."** b. **The nurse replied, "the patient is feeling better."** Which sentence is correct? _____ 2049
Christians, Jews, Thanksgiving Day 2235	**We saw "mutiny on the bounty" at the Mercury theater.** _____ 2236

S V people water DO lawns 173	Find the subject, verb, and direct object in each sentence and write them in the proper blanks: **The heavy rain flooded the street.** S V DO _____ _____ _____ 174
verb 361	a. **came** *from* **Alaska** b. **boy** *from* **Alaska** In which sentence does the preposition *from* relate the noun **Alaska** to a verb? ____ 362
ran 549	PRESENT: **The children** *run* **to the window.** If you changed this sentence from present to past, you would need to change the verb *run* to _____. 550
did 737	**In desperation, he decided to go next door to get advice from another young mother, whom the Dotys had** _____ **(*know*) for several years.** 738
wakes 925	**One of his front teeth (*were, was*) missing.** 926
anybody 1113	**I (*can, can't*) hardly remember when I last saw Andy.** 1114

while 1301	Underline one clause signal that could start an adverb clause that answers the question *Where?* **when** **after** **wherever** 1302
a 1488	Here are two more sentences to be combined: a. **The Fords took care of our dog.** b. **They are our neighbors.** Sentence *b* identifies the _____ in sentence *a*. 1489
fish. Therefore 1675	**It was a small cabin in the upper part of the state.** _____ 1676
team, seems, 1862	**However I shall let you know by Monday if possible. (2)** 1863
a 2049	In this and the following frames, supply the missing commas, periods, and quotation marks: **The waiter said We bake our own pies** 2050
"Mutiny . . . Bounty," Theater 2236	**My dad generally uses dyno gasoline in his pontiac car** _____ 2237

S V rain flooded DO street 174	The story started a good discussion. S V DO _____ _____ _____ 175
a 362	a. **disappeared** *between* **the houses** b. **the fence** *between* **the houses** In which sentence does the preposition *between* relate the noun **houses** to a verb? ____ 363
ran 550	PRESENT SIMPLE PAST PAST WITH HELPER **run** **ran** **(have) run** Write the two different past forms of **run**: I _____ to see where our dog *had* _____. 551
known 738	"You should have _____ (*come*) over earlier," she said. "Just bring the little dear over, and I'll take care of her until Lois and Jim get home." 739
was 926	The leaves of the tree (*are, is*) turning yellow. 927
can 1114	After riding on the roller coaster, we were so dizzy that we (*could, couldn't*) scarcely stand up. Note to student: You are now ready for Unit Test 5. *page 349* 1115

wherever 1302	Underline one clause signal that could start an adverb clause that answers the question *Why?* **although because until** 1303
Fords 1489	**They are our neighbors.** To change this sentence to an appositive word group, drop the two words _____. 1490
cabin in 1676	**My uncle John was working he couldn't go with us.** _____ 1677
However, Monday, 1863	**No our second game as a matter of fact was even worse than the first. (3)** 1864
The waiter said, "We bake our own pies." 2050	**We bake our own pies said the waiter** 2051
Dyno, Pontiac 2237	**The Madison study club heard a talk by professor Norris on negro music.** _____ 2238

S V story started DO discussion 175	The people of Athens governed themselves. S V DO ———————— ———————— ———————— 176

a
 	
363
	There are dozens of prepositions. Here is a list of the nine we most frequently use:
	
	    in at to
	    for on from
	    of with by
	
	How many of these have only two letters? ———————
	
	364

ran, run 551	a. The club ... out of money. b. The club *has* ... out of money. In which sentence would *run* be correct? ———— 552
come 739	After Grandfather Brooks had ———————————— (*take*) the baby to the neighbors' house, he went back to the Dotys' home. 740
are 927	The traffic on our streets (*increase, increases*) every year. 928
could 1115	UNIT 6: CHOOSING THE RIGHT PRONOUN Lesson **38** **Recognizing Subject and Object Forms** [Frames 1117-1140]

because 1303	Underline one clause signal that could start an adverb clause that answers the question *On what condition?* **where as though if** 1304
They are 1490	**The Fords,** *our neighbors,* **took care of our dog.** We have now put the appositive word group next to the noun _____, which it explains. 1491
working. He 1677	**He would join us on Saturday the first day of his vacation.** _____ 1678
No, game, fact, 1864	Lesson **65** **Commas in Addresses and Dates** [Frames 1866-1891]
"We bake our own pies," said the waiter. 2051	**The dentist said Don't eat so many sweets** 2052
Study Club, Professor, Negro 2238	**At the time of this incident, general Burke was only a sergeant.** _____ 2239

S   V

S V people governed DO themselves 176	**A little paint would improve this house.** S V DO _____ _____ _____ (two words) 177
six 364	**We always rode .?. school.** Circle two of these prepositions that would fit into the above sentence: in at to for on from of with by 365
b 552	PRESENT SIMPLE PAST PAST WITH HELPER give gave (have) given Is the simple past form the same as the present form? (*Yes, No*) 553
taken 740	**It was now eleven o'clock, and he had _____ (*grow*) quite sleepy.** 741
increases 928	**One of your tires (*are, is*) flat.** 929
	a. *Fred* **likes** *dogs.* b. *Dogs* **like** *Fred.* In sentence *a*, the noun *Fred* is the subject, and the noun *dogs* is the direct object. In sentence *b*, the noun _____ is the subject, and the noun _____ is the direct object. 1117

if

Now let's look at a one-word adverb again:

The car started *suddenly.*
Suddenly **the car started.**

Can an adverb sometimes be moved from one position to another in a sentence? (*Yes, No*)

Fords

Notice the difference between an appositive and an adjective clause. An adjective clause always has a subject and a verb. An appositive does not.

a. **The Fords,** *who are our neighbors,* **took care of our dog.**
b. **The Fords,** *our neighbors,* **took care of our dog.**

Which sentence contains an appositive? ____

Saturday, the

Since we had never been there before   Uncle John gave us directions.

_____

An address can have one or more parts:

a. **We moved to** *86 Bay Avenue* **last fall.**
b. **We moved to** *86 Bay Avenue, Atlanta,* **last fall.**

In which sentence does the address have more than one part? ____

The dentist said,
"Don't eat so
many sweets."

Today is my birthday   announced Jerry

General

The Merritt library probably has more than one copy of *a man for the ages.*

_____

S paint V would improve DO house 177	**A thick fog covered the entire city.** S V DO _____ _____ _____ 178

Any two:
to, from, at, by
 	
365
	I worked .?. my dad.
	
	Circle two of these prepositions that would fit into the above sentence:
	
	     in at to
	     for on from
	     of with by
	
	366

No 553	The simple past form of *give* is not *give* but _____. 554
grown 741	**He _____ (*lie*) down on the sofa and soon fell asleep.** 742
is 929	**One of the dogs (*looks, look*) like Trixie.** 930
Dogs, Fred 1117	a. *Fred* **likes** *dogs*. b. *Dogs* **like** *Fred*. Is the form of a noun the same whether it is in the subject or direct object position? (*Yes, No*) 1118

Yes

1305

My dog comes *when I call him.*
When I call him, **my dog comes.**

Can an adverb clause be moved from the end to the beginning of a sentence? (*Yes, No*)

1306

---

b

1492

In this and the following frames, change each italicized sentence to an appositive word group. Then put it after the word it explains in the other sentence. Remember that an appositive word group does not have a subject and a verb.

I read the life of Edison. *He was the great inventor.*

_____

1493

---

before, Uncle

1679

The cabin would be easy to find   **it was the fourth cabin beyond a certain road.**

_____

1680

---

b

1866

a. **We moved to** *86 Bay Avenue* **last fall.**
b. **We moved to** *86 Bay Avenue, Atlanta,* **last fall.**

In *a*, the address consists of one part, the street address. In *b*, the address consists of two parts, the *street address* and the _____.

1867

"Today is my birthday," announced Jerry.

2053

You didn't leave any cake for me   **complained Don**

2054

Library,
A Man ... Ages

2240

The Panama canal was begun by the french and completed by the americans.

_____

2241

S V fog covered DO city 178	A direct object _____ the action of the verb or shows the _____ of this action. 179
Any two: for, with, by, on 366	**We stayed .?. a motel.** Circle two of these prepositions that would fit into the above sentence: in at to for on from of with by 367
gave 554	Write the correct past form of **give:** **My uncle _____ me his old typewriter.** 555
lay 742	**Around midnight, the Dotys _____ (come) home from the movie.** 743
looks 930	**The design of the cars (has, have) been improved.** 931

Yes
 	
1118
	Let's use pronouns instead of nouns in the sentences:
	    a. *He* **likes** *them.*
	    b. *They* **like** *him.*
	When sentence *a* is turned around, the pronoun *He* changes to _____, and the pronoun *them* changes to
	
	_____.
	
	1119

As I entered the door,   the tardy bell rang.

Each of these two word groups has a subject and a verb, but the adverb clause does not make sense by itself. The adverb clause is the (*first, second*) word group.

1307

I read the life of Edison, the great inventor.

1493

Potatoes were a failure that year. *They are our main crop.*

_____

_____

1494

---

find. It

1680

We started early in the morning   arriving late in the after-noon.

_____

1681

---

city (town)

1867

a. **We moved to** *86 Bay Avenue* **last fall.**
b. **We moved to** *86 Bay Avenue, Atlanta,* **last fall.**

We use commas when the address has (*one, more than one*) part.

1868

"You didn't leave any cake for me," complained Don.

2054

The little boy explained the broken window to the policeman by saying   I was cleaning my slingshot, and it went off

2055

Canal, French, Americans

2241

There are a catholic church and a hospital close to the Franklin high school.

_____

2242

receives, result 179	Must every action verb be followed by a direct object? (*Yes, No*) 180
Any two: in, at, by 367	It rained .?. the game. All the following words can be used as prepositions. Underline three that would fit in the above sentence: **before below during with after about** 368
gave 555	PRESENT: **Joe's parents** *give* **him too much help.** If you changed this sentence from present to past, you would need to change the verb *give* to _____. 556
came 743	**Lois immediately _____ (*run*) upstairs to check on the baby.** 744
has 931	**The causes of this disease (*are, is*) not known.** 932
him, They 1119	a. *He* **likes** *them.* b. *They* **like** *him.* Are the forms of these pronouns the same whether they are in the subject or direct object position? (*Yes, No*) 1120

first 1307	As <u>I</u> entered the door, the tardy <u>bell rang</u>. The adverb clause starts with the clause signal _____ and ends with the word _____. 1308
Potatoes, our main crop, were a failure that year. 1494	**My uncle brought me a gift.** *It was a leather wallet.* _____ _____ 1495
morning, arriving 1681	**When we entered the cabin we found it in very bad condition.** _____ 1682
more than one 1868	**We moved to** *86 Bay Avenue, Atlanta,* **last fall.** We put commas both *before* and *after* the (*first, second*) part of the address. 1869
The little boy . . . saying, "I was cleaning my slingshot, and it went off." 2055	Lesson **72** More Hints on Quotations [Frames 2057-2084]
Catholic, High School 2242	**The committee consists of major Patton, judge Ryan, and a doctor.** _____ 2243

Lesson **7** Unit Review

[Frames 182-208]

---

before, during,
after

368

Underline the preposition:

I bought a pound of butter.

369

PRESENT	SIMPLE PAST	PAST WITH HELPER
give	gave	(have) given

gave

Write the correct past forms of **give**:

Bill _____ **me the ticket that Dave** *had* _____
to him.

556

557

---

ran

When she _____ (*see*) **that both the baby and the basket
were gone, she let out a scream.**

744

745

---

are

Fred (*doesn't, don't*) **live there any more.**

932

933

No

a. *Paul* **admired** *Jane.*
b. *He* **admired** *her.*

In which sentence would you need to change the italicized words if you turned the sentence around? ____

1120

1121

As ... door

When you remove an adverb clause from a sentence, a complete sentence should remain.

(*When he received the warning.*) **the pilot changed his course.**

Read this sentence without the clause. Are the remaining words a sentence? (*Yes, No*)

My uncle brought me a gift, a leather wallet.

Decker hit a home run. *He is our catcher.*

_____

_____.

---

cabin, we

The roof had been leaking   the walls were peeling.

_____

---

second

We moved to *86 Bay Avenue, Atlanta, Georgia 30311,* **last fall.**

Now the address consists of three parts: the *street address*, the *city*, and the _____, with the Zip Code.

"The dog has been fed," said Mother.

Between the quotation and the **he said** expression, we use a (*comma, period*).

Major, Judge

The Fairfax hotel overlooks lake Arrowhead.

_____

In this unit, we have studied three different kinds of words: nouns, pronouns, and verbs.

A noun is a word used to _____ a person, place, thing, or idea.

182

---

of

369

Underline the preposition:

Everyone looked at her hat.

370

---

gave, given

557

My friend *gave* **me his promise.**

If you added the helper *has* to the verb, you would need to change *gave* to _____.

558

---

saw

745

She _____ (*fly***) downstairs and awoke Grandfather Brooks.**

746

---

doesn't

933

(Doesn't, Don't) **your ears feel frozen?**

934

---

b

1121

.?. admired Jane.

Underline the pronoun in each pair that would fit in the subject position in the above sentence:

I—me, he—him, she—her, we—us, they—them

1122

Yes 1309	**The weather is chilly although this is June.** The adverb clause starts with the clause signal _____ and ends with the word _____. 1310
Decker, our catcher, hit a home run. 1496	**The stories were judged by Mrs. Dix.** *She is a newspaper writer.* _____ _____. 1497
leaking. The 1683	**Several windows were broken and rain had come in.** _____ 1684
state 1870	Note that the state and Zip Code are *not* separated by a comma, as are other parts of the address. Punctuate this sentence: **Please mail the package to me at 110 State Street Detroit Michigan 48223.** 1871
comma 2057	Now let's change the quotation to a question, omitting the punctuation: **Has the dog been fed asked Mother** The entire sentence is not a question. Only the quotation is a question. Therefore, the question mark should be put after the word (*fed, Mother*). 2058
Hotel, Lake 2244	**My aunt took care of my grandfather after he returned home from the Oakhurst hospital.** _____ 2245

name	To avoid repeating a noun, we often use a _____ in its place.
182	183

at	Underline the preposition: **The bridge across the river was closed.**
370	371

given	a. **come run give** b. **came ran gave** Which forms of these verbs show simple past time? ____
558	559

flew	**"The baby—the baby!" she screamed. "Someone has** **_____ (***take***) her away!"**
746	747

Don't	**A cactus (***doesn't, don't***) need much water.**
934	935

I, he, she, we, they	a. **I, he, she, we, they** b. **me, him, her, us, them** In which group are the pronouns that fit in the subject position? ____
1122	1123

although . . . June

1310

We put up our tent   where the ground was dry.

The adverb clause starts with the clause signal _____

and ends with the word _____.

1311

The stories were
judged by
Mrs. Dix, a
newspaper writer.

1497

The fire was discovered by Mr. Olin. *He is the watchman.*

_____

_____.

1498

---

broken, and

1684

We decided to surprise Uncle John   by fixing up the cabin
for him.

_____

1685

Street, Detroit,

1871

Punctuate this sentence:

You can reach us at 2206 Parkside Boulevard Phoenix Arizona 85005 after next Monday.

1872

---

fed

2058

a. "Has the dog been fed?" asked Mother.
b. "Has the dog been fed," asked Mother?

In which sentence is the question mark correctly placed?

____

2059

Hospital

2245

The Hudson river follows the Catskill mountains for many miles.

_____

2246

pronoun 183	Which is usually more definite in meaning, a noun or a pronoun? A _____. 184
across 371	Underline the preposition: Jimmy agreed with his friends. 372
b 559	Write the correct past forms of **come:** My little brother _____ downstairs to see who *had* _____ to our house. 560
taken 747	Grandfather _____ (*sit*) up, still dazed with sleep. 748
doesn't 935	My teeth (*was, were*) chattering from the cold. 936
a 1123	Paul admired .?.. Underline the pronoun in each pair that would fit in the direct object position in the above sentence: I—me, he—him, she—her, we—us, they—them 1124

where ... dry

1311

When Skippy got the ball,   he ran toward the wrong goal.

The adverb clause starts with the clause signal _____

and ends with the word _____.

1312

The fire was discovered by Mr. Olin, the watchman.

1498

Two boys didn't finish the race. *They were Pete and Alvin.*

_____

_____.

1499

John by

1685

We went to the village store   where we bought paint, glass, and tar paper.

_____

1686

Boulevard, Phoenix, Arizona 85005,

1872

Mrs. R. V. Prentis of *461 Archdale Avenue* won the car.

How many parts does this address have? _____

1873

---

a

2059

"The dog has been fed," said Mother.
"Has the dog been fed?" asked Mother.

When we change the quotation to a question, we change

the comma to a _____ mark.

2060

River, Mountains

2246

Our club is planning a party for the last friday in april.

_____

2247

noun 184	a. trees, desk, lamp, Ralph, potatoes b. they, some, each, you, these, several In which group can the words be used as pronouns? ____ 185
with 372	Underline the preposition: **Mr. Fritz usually travels by plane.** 373
came, come 560	Write the correct past forms of **come:** **This package must** *have* _____ **before my parents** _____ **home.** 561
sat 748	**"Oh, yes," he said, "I guess I'm not a very good baby-sitter.** **The baby wouldn't stop crying; so I** _____ *(take)* **her** **over to Mrs. Graham's house."** 749
were 936	**You** *(was, were)* **out when I telephoned.** 937
me, him, her, us, them 1124	a. **I, he, she, we, they** b. **me, him, her, us, them** In which group are the pronouns that fit in the direct object position? ____ 1125

When ... ball

1312

Ralph jumped   as though he had received an electric shock.
The adverb clause starts with the clause signal (two words) _____ and ends with the word _____.

1313

Two boys, Pete and Alvin, didn't finish the race.

1499

We spent a week in Boston. *It is a very historical city.*
_____
_____.

1500

---

store, where

1686

We repaired the windows   then we patched the roof.
_____

1687

---

one

1873

Mrs. R. V. Prentis of *461 Archdale Avenue* **won the car.**
What preposition ties in the address with the name that it follows? _____

1874

---

question

2060

"The dog has been fed," said Mother.
"Has the dog been fed?" asked Mother.
When the quotation is a question, do we use a comma in addition to the question mark? (*Yes, No*)

2061

Friday, April

2247

Follow Elson avenue until you reach Magnolia park.
_____

2248

b 185	In this and the next three frames, each sentence contains two italicized nouns and one italicized pronoun. Underline the one pronoun: *They* **filled the** *box* **with** *ice*. 186
by 373	Underline the preposition: **The rain came into the room.** 374
come, came 561	Write the correct past forms of **run**: **Don** _____ **for the same office for which his brother** *had* _____ **.** 562
took 749	**Lois** _____ (*give*) **a sigh of relief and started out the door.** 750
were 937	(*Here are, Here's*) **the eggs for the cake.** 938
b 1125	Here the subject and object forms of the pronouns are mixed up. Underline the *five* pronouns that could come before the verb as its subject: **they us him I he them me we she her** 1126

as though ... shock 1313	Because Mother loves birds, we gave her a parakeet for her birthday. The adverb clause starts with the clause signal _____ and ends with the word _____. 1314
We spent a week in Boston, a very historical city. 1500	Lesson **52** Unit Review [Frames 1502-1525]
windows. Then 1687	After we painted the walls we scrubbed the floors. _____ 1688
of 1874	a. **Mrs. R. V. Prentis of** *461 Archdale Avenue* **won the car.** b. **Mrs. R. V. Prentis,** *461 Archdale Avenue*, **won the car.** In which sentence is the address put right after the name with no preposition to tie it in? ____ 1875
No 2061	a. **"Has the dog been fed?," asked Mother.** b. **"Has the dog been fed?" asked Mother.** Which sentence is correct? ____ 2062
Avenue, Park 2248	**In february, my grandmother and one of my uncles plan to visit aunt Carol.** _____ Note to student: You are now ready for Unit Test 11, to be followed by the Final Test. 2249

They 186	Underline the one pronoun: *Lyle* **gave** *it* **to a** *friend.* 187
into 374	Underline the preposition: **The book about ants was interesting.** 375
ran, run 562	Write the correct past forms of **run:** **The car _____ better than it ever** *had* **_____ before.** 563
gave 750	## Lesson **25** Unit Review [Frames 752-773]
Here are 938	**There (***are, is***) thirteen countries in South America.** 939
they, I, he, we, she 1126	This time, underline the five pronouns that could come *after* the verb as its direct object: **he them her I us they me we she him** 1127

Because ... birds 1314	**If I don't study this afternoon, I must stay home tonight.** The adverb clause starts with the clause signal _____ and ends with the word _____. 1315
	Do both a sentence and a clause have a subject and a verb? (*Yes, No*) 1502
walls, we 1688	**You could hardly recognize the cabin Uncle John would be surprised.** _____ 1689
b 1875	a. **Mrs. R. V. Prentis of** *461 Archdale Avenue* **won the car.** b. **Mrs. R. V. Prentis,** *461 Archdale Avenue,* **won the car.** When there is no preposition to tie in the address with the name, do we surround it with commas? (*Yes, No*) 1876
b 2062	Now punctuate this sentence yourself: **Has the dog been fed asked Mother** 2063
February, Aunt 2249	*page 374*

it 187	Underline the one pronoun: **The** *boy* **put** *some* **in the** *bank.* 188
about 375	A preposition is a word that shows _____ *ship.* 376
ran, run 563	Write the correct past forms of **give:** **Mr. Carter** *has* _____ **me a higher grade than he** _____ **me last semester.** 564
	In this and the following frames, underline the correct verb in each pair. After any form of **have** or **be,** be sure to select the helper form of the verb. **We had** (*taken, took*) **the wrong road and had** (*ran, run*) **out of gas.** 752
are 939	(*There are, There's*) **no ink in this pen.** 940

them, her, us,
me, him
 	
1127
	The pronouns *you* and *it* are different from the other pronouns.
	
	      a. *You* **followed** *it.*
	      b. *It* **followed** *you.*
	
	Do the pronouns *you* and *it* change in form when they are shifted from subject to direct object? (*Yes, No*)
	
	1128

INDEX

Each entry is indexed by frame number, followed by the page, in parentheses, on which the frame appears. The references included in each entry direct the reader to Key frames. Additional information and related exercises may be found in the frames preceding and following those listed. Complete review exercises for major topics are listed in the table of contents.

E
F
G
H
I
J

9
0
1
2
3